Reflections on XLA

IT service experience and its management as part of ITSM

Mark Smalley

Reflections on XLA

IT service experience and its management as part of ITSM

Mark Smalley

First edition, October 2023
ISBN 9798860754423
Copyright © Mark Smalley, 2023; all rights reserved

COBIT™ is a registered trade mark of ISACA
IT4IT™ is a registered trade mark of The Open Group
ITIL® is a registered trade mark of Axelos Ltd
SIAM™ is a registered trade mark of EXIN
VeriSM™ is a registered trademark of IFDC
XLA® is a registered trade mark of Giarte
SxLA® is a registered trade mark of ESM-groep

Other books in this 'Reflections' series on Amazon:
- Reflections on High-velocity IT
- Reflections on IT Paradigmology
- Reflections on Product to Value

Commissioned books:
- IT4IT™ for Managing the Business of IT – Management Guide (Executive Summary)
- ITIL® 4 High-velocity IT (Lead Editor)
- ITIL® 4 Acquiring and Managing Cloud Services (Chapter 4)
- ITIL® 4 High-velocity IT Reference and Study Guide
- XLA Pocketbook (Content Editor)
- ITSM Value Streams (Chapter 1)

The figures in this paperback version are monochrome. If you would like a free pdf of the colour versions, please send a request to mark@smalley.it.

Table of Contents

Preface 7

Prologue 8

Introduction and summary 11

1. XLA 16

2. Service 22

   2.1 Service 22

   2.2 Service ontology 24

   2.3 Service-dominant logic 27

3. Service experience 29

   3.1 Importance of experience 29

   3.2 Service interactions 31

   3.3 Value from service and its measurement 33

   3.4 Empathy, compassion and expectations 34

4. IT service 35
    4.1 IT services 35
    4.2 Portfolios and catalogues 36
    4.3 Service level agreements 36

5. IT service management 39
    5.1 IT service management 39
    5.2 Positioning 40
    5.3 A generic ITSM framework 42

6. IT service experience 48
    6.1 IT service suffering 48
    6.2 Failed IT state 51
    6.3 IT's reputation paradox 53
    6.4 Both sides matter 55

7. IT service experience management 57
    7.1 Engagement 60
    7.2 Preparation 64
    7.3 Co-creation 66
    7.4 Evolution 71

Epilogue 82

Appendices 83

A.1 A stack of IT system components 84

A.2 Is the what worth the how? 88

A.3 An atlas of negative IT service emotions 92

A.4 XLA behaviour levels 94

A.5 Experience and impact commitment clause 99

A.6 Surveys and alternatives 101

A.7 Changing perceptions of XLA 105

A.8 Other XLA publications 108

Acknowledgements 112

Preface

My exposure to XLA®[1] started in 2018 when I asked Marco Gianotten whether he would like to contribute to the forthcoming radical update of ITIL® – ITIL 4. I thought that his new initiative around XLA would support the more progressive perspective that the ITIL project team was taking to 'service'. He agreed and XLA is mentioned in various parts of ITIL 4, including the ITIL 4 High-velocity IT module for which I had been engaged to create.

In 2020, Marco asked me to help his company Giarte in Amsterdam with the development of their XLA Academy. This resulted in an engagement in the cool role of 'Yoda Master'. I was also content editor for the XLA Pocketbook – Giarte's interpretation of XLA.

During this period, I met Alan Nance, who was on a similar mission. and learned about his interpretation of XLA. I also spoke (and still speak) with HappySignals. They launched their IT experience management platform in 2015 and their thinking about the field is consistent with Marco's and Alan's, and to Bright Horse's, that is successfully building on Alan's work.

With the increasing interest for XLA more parties entered the XLA space. As with all emerging topics, there is divergence of thought as to what XLA is, yet, although sometimes confusing, these differences are beneficial for the development of the field.

Based on this exposure to XLA, I wrote this little book to help people better understand the topic. It is my current understanding of XLA and includes some original thinking, but much of it reflects what I have gratefully learned from my esteemed industry colleagues.

---

[1] XLA is an abbreviation of experience level agreement and is closely related to SLA (service level agreement).

Prologue

Setting the scene

Stage Play

Title: "Metamorphosis in IT: From Frustration to Collaboration"

Act 1 Frustration

Description: In the first act, we find ourselves in a bustling office environment where an uncaring IT service provider is about to undergo a remarkable metamorphosis into a valued partner. Frustration is brewing as a user of IT services encounters issues with the service desk. This scene sets the stage for a journey of change and transformation that will unfold throughout the play.

Scene 1: A busy office with cubicles and an IT service desk. Employees are hard at work, and the IT service agent is stationed at the service desk. The IT service manager just happens to be in the vicinity of the user, and observes from a distance as the story begins.

Characters:

- User (U)
- IT service agent (SA)
- IT service manager (SM)

[U is at their desk, trying to work on a malfunctioning computer. Frustration grows on their face as they repeatedly click the mouse, but nothing happens.]

U: (Muttering to themselves) This is ridiculous! I can't get any work done with this computer acting up.

[U decides to call the IT service desk for help, takes out their phone, and dials the number. The service agent answers the call.]

SA: (Monotonously) IT service desk, how can I help you?

```
U: (Annoyed) Hi, yes, my computer is acting up again.
It's slow, freezing, and I can't get anything done.

SA: (Impersonal) Please provide me with your employee
ID and a brief description of the issue.

[U provides the information, frustrated by the lack of
empathy from the service agent.]

U: (Angrily) Alright, I gave you the details. Can you
please fix it quickly? I have deadlines to meet.

[Exit SA, pursued by a perverse incident resolution
target.]²
```

[End of excerpt]

The scenario in this play sadly resonates with the daily struggles faced by users of IT systems and services. It's a role they never willingly auditioned for – one where technology often falters, and the so-called IT professionals and their managers seem to have lost the plot. This frustrating combination not only disrupts business operations, leading to adverse impacts on productivity, but it also takes an emotional toll on employees due to their experiences with both technology and the professionals meant to support it.

Many IT service managers acknowledge this sorry state of affairs and feel morally obliged to act. They are now turning towards XLA – experience level agreement – not just as a way of working and a way of thinking, but also as something that embodies their desire to be perceived as empathic, responsive and trustworthy.

---

[2] A nerdy reference to one of the most famous of Shakespeare's stage directions, 'Exit, pursued by a bear' in Act III of The Winter's Tale, where Antigonus meets death in the most unlikely of ways: by a bear. While Shakespeare's stage direction symbolizes the unpredictability of life's challenges and fate, the version in this play serves as a metaphor for the challenges faced by IT service professionals, where the pursuit represents both absurdity and the relentless pressure of having to meet dysfunctional targets that undermine true user satisfaction.

These forward-thinking IT service managers see through the hype around XLA. Although XLA offers some potentially disruptive guidance (for example, valuing subjective satisfaction over traditional objective metrics like system uptime and response times), they view it as way of gradually enhancing their IT service management approach by selectively adopting and adapting XLA elements to align with their specific circumstances.

Introduction and summary

Structure of the book

Because XLA (Chapter 1) is an integral part of IT service management, this book first explores service (Chapter 2) and experience (Chapter 3) in general, and IT service (Chapter 4) and its management (Chapter 5) in particular, before reflecting on IT service experience (Chapter 6) and its management (Chapter 7). There are also appendices that some chapters refer to for more detail.

[Figure: Venn-style diagram showing 2. Service, 3. Service experience, 4. IT service, 6. IT service experience, 1. XLA, 5. IT service management, 7. IT service experience management]

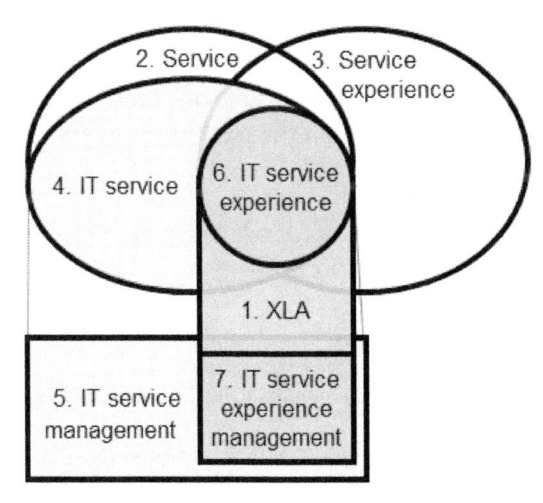

Figure: an 'ontology of contents' – how the chapter topics are interrelated

The content of Chapters 2-5 focuses on aspects of service, experience, IT service and its management that are relevant for IT service experience and its management.

Chapters 1-6 are mostly about understanding the various topics and offer little practical guidance other than the implicit recommendation to consider the consequences of any new perspectives that are mentioned. Chapter 7 (IT service experience management) is not only about understanding what IT service experience management entails. It also offers some practical guidance as to how to manage IT service experience. It is by far the largest chapter.

As such, readers who are looking for practical guidance and have a basic understanding of the topics in Chapters 2-6 can skip or speed-read these chapters. They should, however, realize that the guidance in Chapter 7 may be misinterpreted – for better or for worse – without the context that the previous chapters provide.

In addition, the guidance should be interpreted as 'this *might* work for you' and should always be assessed against the reader's specific circumstances and adapted where appropriate. Because circumstances change over time as a result of internal and external actions, guidance that worked in the past might not work now, and vice versa.

This book touches on many topics that are explored in more depth in the publications described in Appendix 8.

Summary of the content

The chapters and their key statements are summarized as follows.

Chapter 1 – XLA briefly introduces XLA and positions it as an integral part of IT service management.

- XLA is an abbreviation of experience level agreement and is closely related to SLA (service level agreement).
- XLA is not only a concrete agreement between service provider and service recipient. It also refers to the abstract and generic concept of agreeing the desired experience from IT services, and, by implication, to facilitating the desired experience.
- The key beliefs behind XLA are: people desire emotional well-being, IT service affects people and their business, IT

service often falls short, XLA can improve the impact of IT service, and IT practitioners feel morally obliged to better serve IT users.

Chapter 2 – Service provides an understanding of the nature of service in general. Chapter 4 describes service in the specific context of IT systems.

- Service is a form of economic exchange based primarily on the application of competences by each party for mutual benefit, rather than on the transfer of ownership of goods.
- It is useful to distinguish between service systems, service offerings, service relationships, service agreements, service interactions, service outputs and service outcomes.
- Service-dominant logic[3] is a framework that explains how organizations co-create value by the application of competences. It contrasts with goods-dominant logic that emerged in the manufacturing area.

Chapter 3 – Service experience proposes a way of thinking about service experience – experience-dominant logic[4].

- People's emotional state and sometimes also their well-being is affected by their experience with services. This should therefore be an important consideration during service design and execution.
- Service interactions take place within the context of a relationship with expectations, with experiences before, during and after the interactions.
- Value from service is experienced subjectively and is therefore difficult to know with certainty.
- Empathy and compassion are key competences that affect service experience.

---

[3] Stephen L. Vargo and Robert F. Lusch, Wikipedia
[4] Mark Smalley, article on LinkedIn

Chapter 4 – IT service describes service in the context of use of IT systems, referring to commonly used terms such as service level agreements. The chapter extends the content of Chapter 2 about service in general.

- IT services comprise the affordance of access to IT systems, and the performance of actions that support their use.
- IT services are documented generically in service portfolios and service catalogues, and more specifically in service level agreements and service request catalogues.
- Service level agreements describe the agreed services and the service quality that may be expected. This is often expressed in terms of fitness for purpose (utility) and fitness for use (warranty).

Chapter 5 – IT service management describes the essence of IT service management so that it can be referred to in Chapter 7 about IT service experience management.

- IT service management aims to ensure that the right IT services are agreed, that all involved parties are aligned with the agreed services, and that the parties collaborate effectively.
- IT service management's positioning in the IT organization is distinct from but related to the other major IT domains: application development and management, infrastructure engineering, and IT operations.
- In terms of activities, IT service management encompasses the *engagement* between service provider and recipient, the *preparation* of necessary resources, the *co-creation* of actual value by both parties, and the *evolution* of the ways of being, thinking and working.

Chapter 6 – IT service experience proposes that people suffer from poor IT service, that the IT industry has much to answer for, and that there is a paradoxical challenge to be valued for 'invisible' IT services. The chapter extends the content of Chapter 3 about service experience in general.

- IT practitioners should start their improvement journey by acknowledging that people suffer from IT service.
- The IT industry has failed miserably in their relationships with user organizations and needs to make amends.
- Smoothly running IT services can lead to underappreciation of the IT function, while – paradoxically – disruptions are not only a reputational risk but also provide an opportunity for reputation enhancement.
- The provider experience is just as important as the customer experience.

Chapter 7 – IT service experience management describes how service experience is managed as an integral part of IT service management as described in Chapter 5. It offers guidance in four areas.

- Engagement: where agreements (XLAs) are made about the desired IT service experience and where expectations are set.
- Preparation: where the appropriate set of people and resources is selected, and where work is organized.
- Co-creation: where people apply their skills and other resources, and where the outcome is measured as well as possible.
- Evolution: where the outcomes are analysed and improvement hypotheses are created, and where experiments are conducted.

1. XLA

This chapter is a concise introduction to XLA, highlighting its pivotal role as an integral part of IT service management.

What is XLA?

XLA – short for experience level agreement – has gained prominence as a term within the sphere of enhancing the perceived quality of IT services. It focuses on improving how IT services affect people and their business activities and therefore results.

Employees desire to do their jobs without much IT-related friction. Seeing as this is often not the case, negatively affecting both their emotional well-being and business results, there is a case for investment in XLA.

Focus on service and interaction

While the perceived quality of IT services is undeniably influenced by the perceived quality of IT systems, XLA's primary focus lies not on the IT systems but on the services that facilitate access to and provide support for the use of these systems. In other words, the focus is on the experience of the operational aspects of the systems rather than how their functionality is experienced.

Similarly, the quality of the service interactions is closely related to the quality of the work behind the scenes, often referred to as the "line of visibility" in ITIL® 4. However, XLA focuses on the touchpoints and other interactions between the service provider and the service recipient.

XLA as part of SLA

The hype around XLA might suggest that it is a standalone entity and an alternative to the service level agreement (SLA) that documents the agreed-upon IT service standards and quality. This is not the case. XLA is intricately connected to SLA and should be seen as an integral component of SLA rather than a separate entity. Both SLA and XLA concern the quality of IT services, where the traditional SLA tends to focus on process and output, while the XLA's focus is on outcome: human experience and business impact.

As documents, SLA's and XLA's can be combined, with an XLA as a part of, or an appendix to, an SLA. If not combined, the common denominator – the specific IT services – should be made clear. XLA's can be used for both internal and external IT services. For external services, they may be part of the contract, although commercial IT service providers – at least their legal departments – are often reluctant to include commitments beyond their circle of control. The likelihood of inclusion depends on the nature of the services and the relationship. The Formal agreements paragraph in Section 7.1 explores this in more detail.

XLA as a concept

An XLA is not only a concrete agreement between service provider and service recipient regarding specific IT services. When used without the grammatical articles "the" or "an", XLA also refers to the abstract and generic concept of agreeing the desired experience from IT services, and facilitating the desired experience. This concept is less ambiguously referred to as IT service experience management or just experience management (sometimes shortened to ITXM and XM).

XLA's role in IT service management

Just as an XLA is an integral part of an SLA, IT service experience management is an integral part of IT service management (ITSM). It is an aspect that is implicitly related to many IT service management activities but may not have received sufficient attention. The value of giving it a distinct name is in making people more aware of the effect of IT services on people and their business.

Key beliefs underpinning XLA

The key beliefs behind XLA are that

- People desire emotional well-being and that this affected by IT service
- IT service often falls short on both human experience and business impact
- XLA can improve IT service and its impact
- The IT industry has much to answer for, and people deserve better
- IT service professionals feel morally obliged to act.

Why
People deserve better IT service

What
Better human experience
More business impact

How
Better agreements, metrics, and service interactions
Outcome-oriented values, skills, processes, and technology
Contrition, conviction and commitment

Figure: the essence of XLA

Key XLA activities

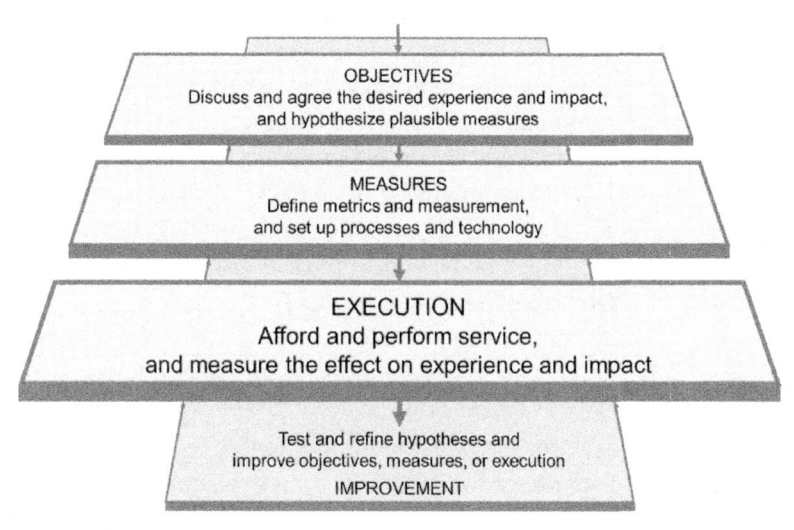

Figure: key XLA activities
(Pyramid diagram levels:)
- OBJECTIVES: Discuss and agree the desired experience and impact, and hypothesize plausible measures
- MEASURES: Define metrics and measurement, and set up processes and technology
- EXECUTION: Afford and perform service, and measure the effect on experience and impact
- IMPROVEMENT: Test and refine hypotheses and improve objectives, measures, or execution

Key XLA terms

This short list comprises some commonly encountered terms[5] related to XLA.

Term	Meaning
DEM	Digital experience monitoring is the monitoring of aspects of IT systems that may affect the end-user experience for employees, customers and other stakeholders. It is often used as a category of applications/platforms for real user monitoring (RUM), endpoint monitoring (EP), and synthetic transaction monitoring (STM).
Experience	The set of emotions, feelings, and judgments that

---

[5] The XLA Pocketbook contains a more comprehensive glossary. The ITIL 4 Glossary contains most IT service management terms.

	arise – in time and over time – from exposure to the presence of or interaction with people and things. This meaning of experience is distinct from other, potentially confusing, meanings: 1. an event that is experienced 2. the experiencing of an event 3. the depth of exposure to something through which knowledge and skills are acquired.
O data	Objective measurements of IT systems, people and interactions.
X data	Subjective measurements of human perception of IT systems, people and interactions.
XI	Experience indicator is a high-level, qualitative or quantitative, representation of experience. It is specified by quantitative metrics based on a combination of X data and O data. In the case of qualitative indicators such as perceived impact of IT on work, the challenge is to identify quantitative metrics with a useful degree of correlation. In practice, indicator and metric are often used interchangeably.
XLA	Experience level agreement is documentation of the desired IT service experience, preferably as part of a service level agreement (SLA). It is also the concept of agreeing the desired experience from IT services, and facilitating the desired experience.
XM	Experience management is the organizational capability for ensuring that the experience of IT services corresponds with expectations to the desired degree. It is sometime referred to as ITXM.

| XMO | Experience management office is an organizational function that stimulates and coordinates the adoption, execution and improvement of experience management. It can be compared with the project management office (PMO) and service management office (SMO). |

2. Service

This chapter provides an understanding of the nature of service in general. Chapter 4 describes service in the specific context of IT systems in three sections:

2.1 Service is a form of economic exchange based primarily on the application of competences by each party for mutual benefit, rather than on the transfer of ownership of goods.

2.2 It is useful to distinguish between service systems, service offerings, service relationships, service agreements, service interactions, service outputs and service outcomes.

2.3 Service-dominant logic is a framework that explains how organizations co-create value by the application of competences. It contrasts with goods-dominant logic that emerged in the manufacturing area.

2.1 Service

In the business context of this book, service is work for one or more other parties in exchange for monetary or non-monetary compensation. Service work is the application of knowledge, skills, and other resources (also known as *performance*, for example, driving somebody from A to B) or the right to use the service provider's resources (also known as *affordance*, for example, renting a car), or both.

Service is the act of integrating and applying competences and other resources by two or more parties within dynamic service ecosystems, with the intent to co-create value, with a focus on relationship-building, and with consideration of the context-dependent, unique and phenomenological nature of value from service.

Services, goods and products

In their purest form, services differ from goods, where ownership of resources change hands. In practice though, products (the collective name for services and goods) are often a mix of services and goods on a goods-services continuum where the proportion of goods-related tangible elements and services-related intangible elements gradually changes. In its simplistic form, the continuum starts with pure goods, moving through core goods with accompanying services, and core services with accompanying goods, to pure services.

Asymmetry

Service is usually asymmetrical, where the provider has more knowledge and plays a more dominant role, and the other plays a more passive role as the recipient[6]. However, the recipient is always responsible for integrating the service into their own processes. This includes the communication of their needs and context to the service provider, and the assessment of the probable effect of the service. Conversely, the provider has an obligation to help the recipient to communicate their needs and context, and to help them understand the probable effect of the service.

When services are offered 'as is', the only reason for communicating needs and context to the provider is to establish the probably effect of the standard service. When providers are unwilling or unable to communicate with individual recipients, it is the recipients' responsibility to assess the probably effect. Conversely, the provider has an obligation to provide generic

---

[6] In addition to *recipient*, this book uses the terms *consumer, customer, user organization,* and *end-user* to denote the party that either acquires and/or uses the service. The context in which the terms are used hopefully clarifies the meaning. The distinction between customer and end-user in explored in Appendix 2 – Is the what worth the how?

information that enables the recipients to assess the suitability (for example, the service's intended purpose, target audience, benefits, possible customization, usage, pricing, guarantees, updates, support, and termination procedure).

2.2 Service ontology

Here is an overview of the key parts of service and their primary relationships. It is intended to help people understand and discuss (IT) service more effectively. Models are by definition selective. They include the parts that are important for the model's goal, and exclude the less relevant parts.

```
┌─────────────────────────────────────────────────────────┐
│  SERVICE PROVIDER                      SERVICE RECIPIENT │
│                       ┌──────────┐                       │
│   People              │ Service  │              People   │
│   influence and       │ offerings│       influence and   │
│   are influenced      └────┬─────┘       are influenced  │
│                           scope                          │
│                       ┌────┴─────┐                       │
│        require        │ Service  │      require          │
│    ┌─────────────────▶│agreements│◀─────────────────┐    │
│    │                  └────┬─────┘                  │    │
│    │                      scope                     │    │
│    ▼                  ┌────┴─────┐                  ▼    │
│ ┌────────┐            │          │            ┌────────┐ │
│ │Service │            │ Service  │            │Service │ │
│ │compo-  │  enable    │inter-    │  enable    │compo-  │ │
│ │nents   │───────────▶│actions   │◀───────────│nents   │ │
│ └────────┘            │          │            └────────┘ │
│  acquire│arrange      └──────────┘            acquire│arrange │
│    ▼                                                ▼    │
│ ┌────────┐    change               change   ┌────────┐   │
│ │Resour- │◀─────────          ─────────────▶│Resour- │   │
│ │ces     │                                  │ces     │   │
│ └────────┘                                  └────────┘   │
│                      Smalley.IT®                         │
│                    Relationships                         │
│              influence and are influenced                │
└─────────────────────────────────────────────────────────┘
```

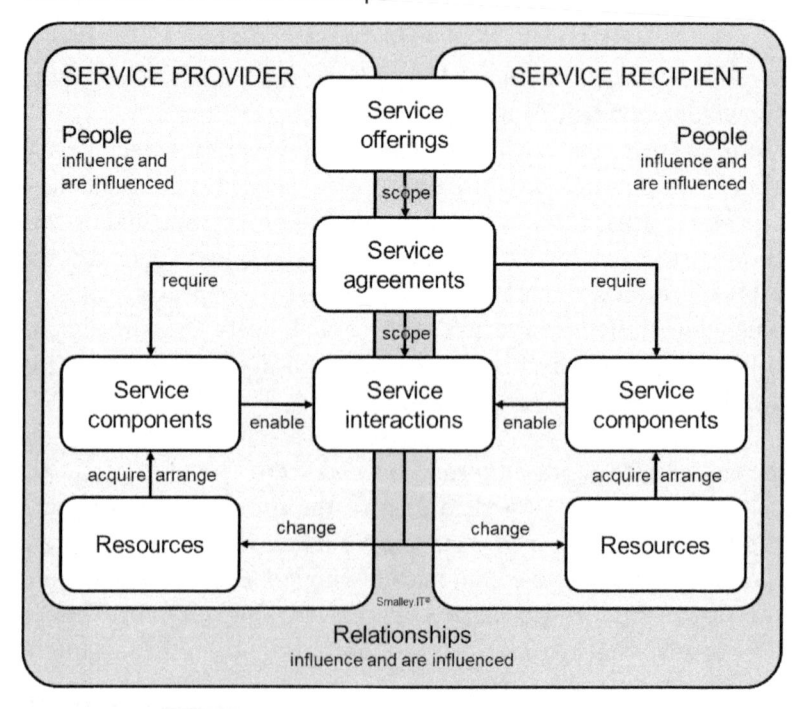

Figure: a service ontology, depicting the interaction between two parties

Included

- The various ways 'service' is used: as a cascade of offerings, agreements and interactions.
- The concept of service components: the 'configuration' of tangible and intangible resources that are dynamically arranged to enable service interaction (for example, people and technology).
- The distinction between service components as resources and the resources that are needed to acquire and arrange the service components: human (for example, values, beliefs, knowledge, skills, relationships), financial, physical, logical (for example, algorithms, software), informational resources.
- The distinction (as made in service-dominant logic) between passive (or 'operand') resources and active (or 'operant') resources: things and people.
- Service interactions that result in changes to (the value of) each party's (or 'service system') resources, the value of which is subjectively determined by the recipient: service as a form of economic exchange.
- Service that happens between people (even when people use other people's technology) who influence and are influenced by both the direct service interactions and other, indirect, encounters (for example, commercial and social brand exposure).
- As a consequence, their relationships that also affect and are affected by the interactions and encounters, the primary aspect of the relationship being trust based on the perception of the other party's ability, integrity, and benevolence (Mayer et al.[7]).

---

[7] An Integrative Model of Organizational Trust, Roger C. Mayer, James H. Davis, F. David Schoorman; article in The Academy of Management Review (1995)

Excluded

The model does not express the useful distinction between output and outcome. This can be imagined as a recursive structure within resources: a service interaction results in a changed resource (output) that is then used to change another resource (outcome).

Neither does the model describe how the resources (boxes) and activities (arrows) are governed, managed and improved: it focuses on the primary process. There are probably other aspects that were unintentionally excluded, for better or for worse.

Relationships

The relationships between most entities in the model are described in terms of a line with the action that the 'higher' entity (blunt end) does to the other (arrow end). For example, the service agreement scopes the service interactions. 'Scope' should be interpreted as constraining but also enabling. The relationships between people and relationships (between people) are not explicit. This would make the model too complicated. It is implicit that people:
- determine the service offering (the provider) and the need for a service offering (the consumer)
- engage and come to a service agreement
- acquire and arrange the required service components
- interact (perform service and afford service) by applying their respective service components
- are affected (emotionally and otherwise) by their perception of the interactions and other encounters
- are affected by their perception of the changed resources as a result of the interactions.

2.3 Service-dominant logic

Service-dominant logic (S-D logic) is a marketing and economic theory that offers a perspective on how economic exchange and value creation occur, particularly in the context of services. According to S-D logic, service is defined in a fundamentally different way compared to the traditional goods-dominant logic. Here's how service is described according to service-dominant logic:

Service as the basis of exchange: In S-D logic, service is seen as the fundamental basis of all economic exchange. This means that all economic activities, including the exchange of goods, are ultimately service-based. When a product is purchased, it is the service or utility provided by that product that creates value for the customer.

Co-creation of value: S-D logic emphasizes that value is not embedded in products or services themselves but is co-created by the interaction between the provider and the customer. Customers actively participate in the value creation process by integrating the service into their own processes and contexts. This highlights the importance of understanding customers' needs, contexts, and experiences in value creation. Customers also actively participate in communicating their needs, requirements and expectations.

Resource-focused: S-D logic places a strong emphasis on resources as the primary drivers of value creation. Resources include not only tangible assets like products but also intangible assets like knowledge, skills, and relationships. The integration and application of these resources by both the service provider and the customer play a central role in value co-creation.

Relationship-oriented: Service-dominant logic recognizes that relationships between service providers and customers are critical to value creation. These relationships are not just transactional but are ongoing, collaborative, and mutually beneficial. Building and maintaining strong customer-provider relationships are central to the success of service-dominant businesses.

Context-dependent: S-D logic acknowledges that the value of a service is context-dependent, meaning that the same service may have different value propositions for different customers in different situations. Understanding the specific needs and context of each customer is essential for effective value creation.

Service ecosystems: S-D logic views markets as complex service ecosystems where multiple actors (service providers, customers, intermediaries, etc.) interact and co-create value together. These ecosystems are dynamic and can adapt to changing circumstances and customer preferences.

Service in service-dominant logic is not limited to traditional notions of service like customer support or hospitality. Instead, it represents the foundational concept of value creation through the integration of resources and the active participation of both service providers and customers in a relationship-based, context-dependent, and resource-focused manner within dynamic service ecosystems. This perspective challenges the conventional view of goods as the primary drivers of value and highlights the centrality of service in modern economies.

From this perspective, service can be defined as the act of integrating and applying competences and other resources by two or more parties within dynamic service ecosystems, with the intent to co-create value, with a focus on relationship-building, and with consideration of the context-dependent, unique and phenomenological nature of value from service.

3. Service experience

This chapter proposes a way of thinking about service experience – experience-dominant logic. It is divided into four sections:

3.1 People's emotional state and sometimes also their well-being is affected by their experience with services. This should therefore be an important consideration during service design and execution.

3.2 Service interactions take place within the context of a relationship with expectations, with experiences before, during and after the interactions.

3.3 Value from service is experienced subjectively and is therefore difficult to know with certainty.

3.4 Empathy and compassion are key competences that affect service experience.

This is based on twelve assertions as proposed as foundational principles of 'experience-dominant logic' that is used by experience-dominant organizations. They are intended as a starting point for consideration and discussion, and will undoubtedly be refined over time.

3.1 Importance of experience

People desire emotional well-being

This is a basic human need. In terms of the Maslow Pyramid, assuming that basic physiological, safety and social needs are met, people feel good when they respect themselves and feel respected by others. Dignity, meaning, purpose, agency and hope contribute to this desirable emotional state.

People's emotions are affected by their experience of people, things and actions

People are affected by:

- what they attend to (gaze),
- what they observe (perception),
- how they feel (conscious and unconscious emotions), and
- what they understand (knowledge, constructs/stories).

Emotions are generally considered to be significant drivers of behaviour. Emotions are influenced, consciously and unconsciously, by external and internal triggers and factors including biological factors. Decisions are often rationalized after the unconscious emotional decision has been made, giving the reassuring illusion of conscious control.

Experience is therefore a major consideration in the design and execution of human-centric products and services

Because experience influences emotions that, in turn, influence decisions and behaviour, organizations should be aware of the emotional effect of their products and services on both providers and consumers. In this context, emotional well-being is either a means to a goal or a goal in its own right. Organizations should be aware how people's emotional states affect how they contribute to non-human goals, for example, profit. Organizations should also have goals regarding the emotional state (usually in terms of happiness) of their employees, customers and other stakeholders. The balance between the various types of goals varies across organizations, industries, cultures etc.

3.2 Service interactions

Service interactions between parties take place within the context of a relationship with expectations about the individual parties and the collective collaboration

When people interact, each party has expectations about how they and the other party will perform, how much effort will be involved, and how effective the collaboration will be. Trust plays an important role in forming expectations about a party. Trust is based on the trustor's perception of the trustee's intentions, integrity, benevolence and 'technical' abilities in relevant domains:

- Intentions are what someone plans to do; when publicly stated, intentions become promises.
- Integrity is how the trustee adheres to acceptable principles such as honesty, openness, reliability and consistency, in particular with respect to their promises.
- Benevolence is whether they do good beyond what is generally expected.
- Trust is also based on whether the trustee demonstrates reciprocal trust and vulnerability by taking risks with behaviour outside their direct scope of control.

Relationships are influenced by direct interactions with the other party, and by indirect encounters with the other party's brand

Relationships are not only based on direct perceptions and observations, for example when discussing, negotiating and executing agreements, but are also influenced by the whole brand experience: indirect touchpoints with manifestations of the provider's brand, including media presence, reviews and recommendations. Before parties actually engage, they each have feelings and thoughts about what to expect from the other party and how the collaboration might be.

Experience is based on individual service interactions, and on the relationship that has been influenced by previous interactions as well as indirect encounters

The experience of a service interaction is influenced by the expectations associated with the relationship. The first service interaction with a party will be compared with the general expectations set by the brand experience and the specific expectations based on discussions and negotiations. The experience of each service interaction will refine the relationship, in particular trust. Subsequent service interactions will be compared with the cumulative experience from previous service interactions.

Experience related to service interactions occurs before, during and after the interaction

The experience of a service interaction starts with the expectation of how it might be (for example, apprehension, based on previous encounters or word of mouth from other parties). It is then recalibrated by the quality of the preparatory interaction (for example, quality of information received, effort required to make arrangements, perceived understanding and empathetic recognition of the situation). Further refinement occurs during the actual service interaction and afterwards, based on the quality of the results and their ease of use and usefulness in achieving the desired outcomes. The experience during each step is influenced by the experience during previous steps and the expected experience during future steps.

Experience related to service interactions is influenced by technical and psychological characteristics of the interaction

A service experience is influenced by objective 'technical' characteristics such as duration as well as how they are psychologically framed. Waiting for 10 minutes for a train with information about the arrival time is usually a better experience than waiting 5 minutes for a train without knowing when it will arrive.

3.3 Value from service and its measurement

Each person experiences a service differently and, for each person, each experience differs

This assertion is closely aligned with service-dominant logic's tenth foundational premise: 'value is always uniquely and phenomenologically determined by the beneficiary'. The key message is that all value propositions are perceived and integrated differently by each actor (all actors are both providers and beneficiaries), meaning that value is uniquely experienced and determined. Value is understood in terms of the holistic and dynamic combination of resources involved.

Experience metrics are always an approximation of actual experience, because they are based on people's reported experience, or on a correlation between behaviour and reported experience

Experience is hard to describe, so much of the actual experience is lost in the individual's own words or their interpretation of other people's words in a survey. They also may be reluctant to share their true or full experience. Reported experience should therefore be regarded as an approximate metric that varies in accuracy. Experience can be inferred from certain behaviour when there is a correlation between that behaviour and reported experience. Because of the uncertainty of the accuracy of reported experience, these behaviour-based metrics of experience are also only approximations that vary in accuracy.

Metric-based monitoring and improvement of experience should therefore incorporate frequent evaluation of the correlation between metrics and indicators with desired outcomes, and experimental changes

Because experience is not only unique to each individual but also varies over time, experience-based metrics should be frequently evaluated against the overarching question whether the what feels worth the how. Because of the emergent and unpredictable behaviour that characterizes service work, experiments should be included in improvement initiatives. It should be noted that monitoring and improvement also influences the experience.

3.4 Empathy, compassion and expectations

The recognition of empathy influences experience for the better

Empathy[8] is the ability to sense signals that cannot be expressed in metrics and to interpret combinations of signals such that people understand or feel what another person is experiencing. For most people, the recognition of empathy in another person is a positive experience that contributes to their emotional well-being. Reciprocally, recognition that empathy has been recognized also benefits the person who expresses empathy.

It is not enough to have empathy and understand the emotions of others. Compassion is also needed in order to take action to help.

The ability to influence expectations should also be recognized, because expectations influence experience. The IT industry has a lot to learn from marketing[9].

---

[8] Empathy is one of the five "RATER" determinants of service quality as used in the GAP/SERVQUAL model. In their usual order of importance, they are reliability, responsiveness, assurance, empathy and tangibles. Hank Marquis explores these in depth in his book Completely Satisfied (seen Appendix 8).

[9] Marketing gurus Seth Godin and Rory Sutherland are great sources of inspiration for framing services more effectively.

4. IT service

This chapter describes service in the context of use of IT systems, referring to commonly used terms such as service level agreements. The chapter extends the content of Chapter 2 about service in general. It is divided into three sections:

4.1 IT services comprise the affordance of access to IT systems, and the performance of actions that support their use.

4.2 IT services are documented generically in service portfolios and service catalogues, and more specifically in service level agreements and service request catalogues.

4.3 Service level agreements describe the agreed services and the service quality that may be expected. This is often expressed in terms of fitness for purpose (utility) and fitness for use (warranty).

4.1 IT services

IT services comprise the affordance of access to the IT systems[10] that provide the users with functionality, and the support of their use of IT systems. They are the bridge between end users and the IT systems that they use. As mentioned in Chapter 1 about XLA, this book is not about the quality of the IT systems, which of course also affect the human experience and business impact, but about the quality of the IT services that provide access to the IT systems. The quality of IT systems and IT services go hand-in-hand. Low IT system quality (for example, uncompromising algorithms that do cover the variety of situations that users encounter, leaving the users frustrated) cannot be compensated by good IT service. Equally valid, good IT systems can be compromised by low

---

[10] Applications, data and infrastructure. Appendix 1 details the underlying stack of components of IT systems.

IT service quality (for example, poor availability and performance, or slow support).

4.2 Portfolios and catalogues

IT services are documented in service portfolios that are usually used internally to keep track of and manage all past, present and future IT services.

Current IT services offerings are documented in service catalogues for specific target audiences, typically those who are involved in acquiring IT services.

Individually contracted IT services are documented in service levels agreements. Service request catalogues are sometimes used to translate the agreed IT services into operational items that users can order under the conditions of the service levels agreement.

Services vary in their degree of standardization, and providers in their desire and ability to deal with customers individually. This is reflected in the agreements and relationships. Balancing standardization and individualization is a strategic decision that service providers make to align with their business goals and target customer segments.

4.3 Service level agreements

Service level agreements (SLA) are self-explanatory: they are agreements about the services and service levels.

While the intent is to document the *expected* level of service, the expectations may deviate (in particular from the service recipient's perspective) from what has been agreed. Non-technical service recipients often do not understand the consequences of service levels such as mean time to restore service that are formulated by, and from the perspective of, the service provider. In many cases, the service recipient accepts the service levels in good faith, assuming that this is just the way things are done in the notoriously nerdy IT industry.

As stated in the XLA Pocketbook, most service level agreements comprise the following parts:

1. **Context**
   - The contract that refers to the SLA (in case of external services)
   - Procedures for the use of services (often as a separate but related document)

2. **Scope**
   - A list and description of the (standard or custom) services to be provided

3. **Service quality levels, metrics, and conditions (generic or per service)**
   - Functionality, for example, operation according to specifications
   - Availability, for example, service window, percentage available, duration of outages, hours of support
   - Performance, for example, reaction time and solution time for service requests
   - Security, for example, effectiveness of prevention of social engineering attacks on systems, time to restore backed-up data

4. **Process**
   - Roles and responsibilities
   - Monitoring
   - Reporting
   - Improvement

Service levels are often categorized in terms of utility (fitness for purpose) and warranty (fitness for use). In the types of service levels mentioned above (in 3), functionality is in the utility category, while availability, performance and security are in the warranty category.
Note that warranty includes the possibility of making agreements about service experience. In practice, however, the agreements focus on objective measurements of the IT system and IT services, rather than subjective measurements of how IT system and IT services, and the IT provider are experienced.

Each service level is described in terms of
- Indicators – for example, speed of handling service calls
- Metrics that specify the indicator – for example, resolution time
- Data for measurement – for example, time stamps in an ITSM system
- Targets for the indicator – for example, 80% of calls within 3 business hours and 90% of calls within 7 business hours.

5. IT service management

This chapter describes the essence of IT service management so that it can be referred to in Chapter 7 about IT service experience management. It is divided into three sections:

5.1 IT service management aims to ensure that the right IT services are agreed, that all involved parties are aligned with the agreed services, and that the parties collaborate effectively.

5.2 IT service management's positioning in the IT organization is distinct from but related to the other major IT domains: application development and management, infrastructure engineering, and IT operations.

5.3 In terms of activities, IT service management encompasses the engagement *between service provider and recipient, the* preparation *of necessary resources, the* co-creation *of actual value by both parties, and the* evolution *of the ways of being, thinking and working.*

5.1 IT service management

IT service management has three main tasks.

Firstly, it ensures that the right IT services are agreed. The services should support the user organization's objectives as much as possible. Within the user organization, there is a principal who determines the requirements for the IT service and is responsible for achieving the desired outcomes. In some cases, the principal and end users are part of the same organization but this is not the case when one company provides IT services (for example, a digital customer service desk) to another company. For more about the principal-agent relationship in the context of XLA, see Appendix 2 – Is the how worth the what?

Secondly, IT service management consults with all involved parties and ensures that they are aligned with the agreed services. These parties can be teams within the internal IT function[11], or can be external parties. The alignment can be achieved by a combination of communication and commitment. Commitment is formalized in an internal or external service level agreement. This alignment is a prerequisite for effective collaboration; otherwise, collaboration may be hindered by parties prioritizing individual targets over shared objectives.

Finally, IT service management ensures that all involved parties collaborate effectively, including IT service management itself. IT service management therefore has both a role in executing its own service activities and coordinating the execution of service activities by other parties. It typically possesses limited direct control over *how* other parties fulfil their roles, such as managing their personnel, processes, resources, and products. However, it does wield a measure of influence over the execution of what has been mutually agreed upon, stemming from its responsibility within the service agreement.

5.2 Positioning

IT service management is a domain that is distinct from, but closely related to, other IT domains. As stated in the previous section, the IT service management function often has no formal authority over the parties responsible for these other domains, yet is tasked with ensuring that these domains are aligned with the IT services that have been agreed with the customer or user organization. IT service management's key capability is coordination.

---

[11] 'IT function' is used in its broader sense and includes application development and management as well as infrastructure engineering, IT operations and IT service management.

Application development is tasked with developing the initial version of application software and major releases, and with transferring it to application management for maintenance and support. Application development and application management are sometimes combined in a software product team.

Infrastructure engineering provides, maintains and supports the platforms and devices that are needed to develop, manage and run the applications. IT operations runs the applications and infrastructure, ensuring performance, security and continuity. Infrastructure engineering and IT operations are sometimes combined in an I&O (infrastructure and operations) function.

IT service management ensures that the right IT services are agreed, that all involved parties are aligned with the agreed services, and that the parties communicate and collaborate effectively. In addition to coordinating the various IT functions, IT service management also coordinates with the customer and user organization. The IT service management function is sometimes added to the I&O function.

User organizations often appoint a part-time super user or create a dedicated functionality management function to liaise with IT service management function regarding the desired IT services. This communication channel often replaces the channel between business/information analysis with application development regarding the functionality after the initial development.

Infrastructure engineering	Application management	IT service management	Functionality management	Business management
		Application development	Business analysis	
IT operations		performances / affordances	Business operations	
Infrastructure	Applications	Services	Information	Improvement

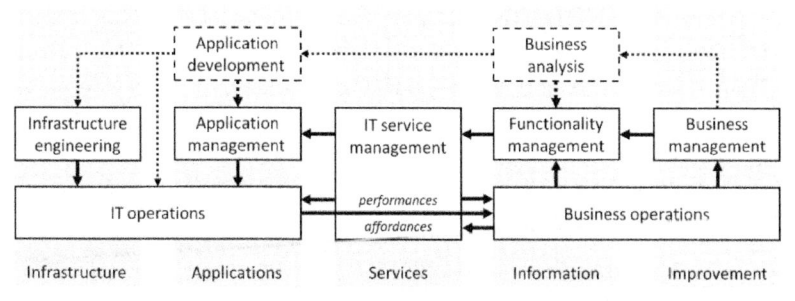

Figure: IT service management and related domains

In addition to the IT services provided to internal or external users by the IT function, the IT function also acquires IT services from external parties and integrates them with other IT services and resources to form the user-facing IT services. This is also IT service management and is executed by both the acquiring party and the providing party, for example by an application team in the IT function and an external cloud service provider that provides a development platform. The integration and management of IT services from multiple parties in the end-to-end value chain is a specific aspect of IT service management that is referred to as service integration and management (SIAM).

5.3 A generic ITSM framework

This paragraph uses the Groovy IT Service Management Framework[12] to illustrate the major areas of knowledge and activity in IT service management. It emerged as a result of exposure to standards and frameworks such as ISO 20000, ITIL®, IT4IT™, VeriSM™, and ISM. It seemed that they could be loosely unified in terms of four areas: engagement, preparation, co-creation and evolution. Evolution is in a different dimension than the other areas, being about the whole of engagement, preparation and co-creation. Each area is described in terms of two key activities and two key topics to understand. Whereas most ITSM frameworks have a strong focus on activities (processes, for example), the thinking here is that there is value in understanding the nature of the 'objects' and the dynamics between the objects that play a role in these areas. This insight enables the practitioner to decide which activities to take. Non-ITSM frameworks (such as BABOK and PMBOK) often describe their field in terms of "knowledge areas", and this term might apply here.

---

[12] https://www.linkedin.com/pulse/groovy-service-management-mark-smalley/

The framework can also be mapped to the GAP[13] model of service quality (previously known as SERVQUAL).

Although the description below starts with engagement, in most cases it will have been preceded by co-creation – possibly in the context of a service from a different provider

And, of course, although the arrow indicates that preparation is related to co-creation, engagement also requires preparation. So, the four areas should be interpreted as types of activities that often occur in the sequence that the arrows indicate, but not always. As always, models are imperfect. But hopefully useful.

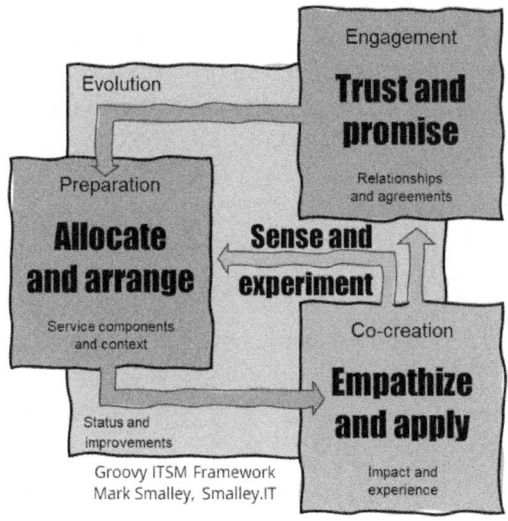

Figure: Groovy IT Service Management Framework

Engagement is where service provider and consumer discover each other's existence and assess both each other's potential contribution and potential relationship. The key activities are **trust** and **promise**.

---

[13] Hank Marquis explores this in his book Completely Satisfied (see Appendix 8).

- Trust manifests itself in the relationship and can be explored in terms of the other party's 'technical' ability, benevolence and integrity, and the alignment of their perceived values with the party's own values.
- Promise is about the interplay between intentions, promises, impositions, obligations, and assessments, resulting in an agreement (refer to Promise Theory[14] for further exploration). The agreement captures the agreed value of the service, which may differ from the value that each party expects.

The key topics are relationships and agreements.

Preparation is where the agreement is translated into the people and resources ("service components") required for the actual service interactions. The key activities are **allocate** and **arrange**.

- Allocate is about identifying and assigning the people and resources to the service.
- Arrange is about organizing them so that they are ready to act or be acted upon during the service interactions.

The key topics are service components and context (because what works in one organizational context may not work in another). Starting with the expected and agreed value, this is transformed into potential value that can be utilized in the next area, co-creation.

Co-creation is where service provider and consumer apply their knowledge, skills and other resources for mutual benefit (this is the service-dominant logic definition of service). The key activities are **empathize** and **apply**.

- **Empathize** is about understanding where the other party is in the service journey, and how they are feeling about it.

---

[14] Mark Burgess

Understanding is not enough, however: it has to be accompanied by compassion that drives people to act.
- **Apply** is about each party using their resources. This is in the form of affordance and performance. Affordance is when you give the other party access to your resources, for example the use of an application. Performance is the application of your resources, for example using your knowledge to skills to explain how a user should use the application.

The key topics are business impact and human experience (of the interaction and the business impact). The potential value present in the arranged service components is transformed into 'kinetic' value when people use (the output of) the service to achieve business results. For example, the business impact when someone acts on a decision that was improved by information that a user derived from an application.

Finally, **evolution** is where the whole of engagement, preparation and co-creation is elevated to a higher level. The key activities are **sense** and **experiment**.

- Sense is about understanding the nature and the status of the organizational system in which service happens. One of the key characteristics is the predictability of the system, in other words the degree of linear causality.
- Plans work in predictable systems, but often the system – particularly when people are involved – is unpredictable. In these cases, it is more effective to experiment and assess how successful the experiments are. The Cynefin sense-making framework offers much guidance in this area.

The key topics are status (of the system) and improvements.

Note that engagement, preparation, co-creation and evolution apply to both service provider and consumer. This emphasizes the co-creational nature of service in which the consumer plays an active and crucial role. The following table illustrates the interplay.

	Service provider	Service consumer
Engagement	Explore market Offer services	Understand needs Identify providers
	Assess potential relationship and agreement Negotiate and agree services Foster relationship Manage and improve agreement	
	Assess value Terminate agreement	Assess value Terminate agreement
Preparation	Assign roles Allocate resources	Assign roles Adjust procedures Integrate service with other systems and services
	Make working agreements Train users Introduce system and services	
	Remove access to system Reallocate team and resources	Transition to new system
Co-creation	Afford access to system Monitor system and services	Use services to process data Use data to achieve outcomes
	Request and provide services	
Evolution	Improve interaction	
	Improve operating and/or business model	Improve operating and/or business model

Standards and frameworks

The following list gives a summary of prominent standards and frameworks that are often used for IT service management, each with their launch date and primary focus, and with Agile, DevOps and XLA as points of reference in the timeline.

- ITIL® (1989) – practices
- COBIT™ (1996) – control
- *Agile (2001) – speed and flexibility of development*
- ISO 20000 (2005) – requirements for the ITSM system
- *DevOps (2009) – speed of deployment*
- SIAM™ (~2010) – integration in the IT supply chain
- IT4IT™ (2015) – data and value streams
- *XLA® (2015) – service experience.*

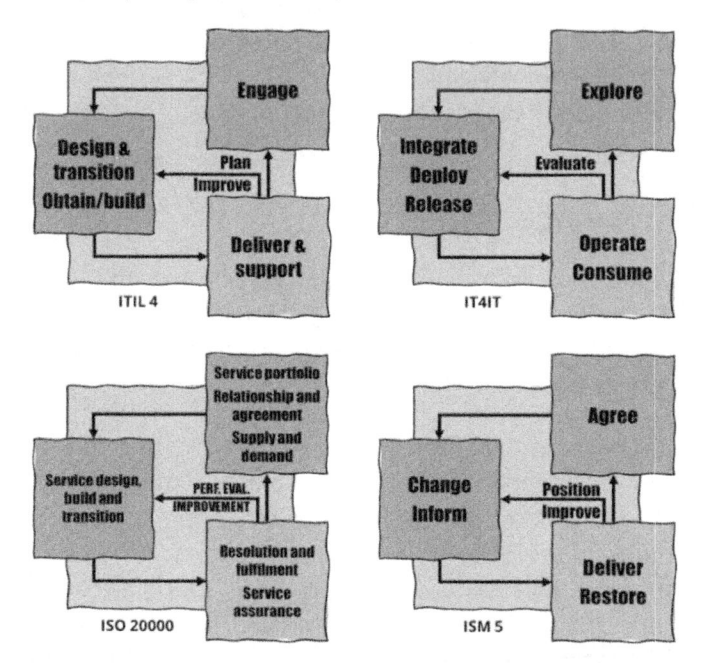

Figure: various ITSM frameworks and standards mapped to the Groovy IT Service Management Framework

6. IT service experience

This chapter proposes that people suffer from poor IT service, that the IT industry has much to answer for, and that there is a paradoxical challenge to be valued for 'invisible' IT services. The chapter extends the content of Chapter 3 about service experience in general. It is divided into four sections:

6.1 IT practitioners should start their improvement journey by acknowledging that people suffer from IT service.
6.2 The IT industry has failed miserably in their relationships with user organizations and needs to make amends.
6.3 Smoothly running IT services can lead to underappreciation of the IT function, while – paradoxically – disruptions are not only a reputational risk but also provide an opportunity for reputation enhancement.
6.4 The provider experience is just as important as the customer experience.

6.1 IT service suffering

This paragraph explores IT-related stress through the lens of an ancient Buddhist concept. It is for people who are concerned about IT's impact on people and their business, and who have the compassion to do something about it.

Old is not necessarily outdated. Old ways of thinking and working sometimes just need to be adapted to a new context. With that in mind, here is an adaption of Buddhism's Four Noble Truths of Suffering to describe suffering in the IT domain. Yes, IT suffering. IT is stressful, for both users and providers. Users are anxious at the mere thought of having to call a service desk. Years after IT engineers have been on pager duty, they get a physiological reaction when a phone buzzes. IT affects people's well-being. We need to take this seriously.

In Buddhism, the Four Noble Truths acknowledge the universal existence of suffering and its root causes. They offer a framework for understanding suffering, its origin in desire and attachment, the possibility of its cessation, and the path to liberation from suffering through mindfulness, self-awareness, and transformative action.

The four noble truths of IT suffering are

1. The truth of IT suffering: IT services have an impact on people's emotional state and sometimes even well being.
2. The truth of the cause of IT suffering: inconsiderate behaviour and uncompromising algorithms.
3. The end of IT suffering: IT suffering is alleviated by a focus on IT's impact on people and their business.
4. The path to the end of IT suffering: acknowledge the existence of IT suffering and apply empathy and compassion to continually improve the experience.

This adaptation is based on experience-dominant logic described in Chapter 3. These four noble truths of IT suffering are described in more detail below. The emphasis is not on product design but rather the services that enable users to benefit from the software, data, and devices.

1. The truth of IT suffering

Just as the First Noble Truth states that suffering is inherent in human existence, in the context of IT service, it acknowledges that suffering often arises from IT service. Users experience frustration from disruptions to their work and from poorly designed or executed service interactions, while providers are stressed from achieving customer satisfaction with limited autonomy, knowledge, and other resources. For examples of negative emotions, see Appendix 3 – Atlas of negative emotions.

In IT we talk about Digital Employee Experience (DEX), in particular with respect to tools that measure IT-related behaviour. DEX enhances survey metrics, which are increasingly problematic. People are fed up with surveys in general, let alone poorly-designed ones that detract from the desired experience. There are also significant intrinsic limitations to surveys: they only survey active and willing customers, not those who have given up, and they are subject to biases. Surveys are explored more in Appendix 6 – Surveys and alternatives. IT functions are therefore increasingly looking at indirect and inferred DEX metrics that complement direct survey metrics.

2. The truth of the cause of IT suffering

The Second Noble Truth suggests that the cause of suffering is desire and attachment. With IT service, the cause is a combination of inconsiderate behaviour and uncompromising algorithms that, in turn, are caused by inconsiderate behaviour. This thoughtlessness is often caused by ignorance of the other party's situation, but can also be affected by constraints and perverse incentives that discourage people from doing the right thing, or by lack of energy and resources. It is seldom due to an individual but rather, an organizational system that leads them to pursue the wrong goal. In other words, it is about inconsiderate management: without deliberately leading with DEX in mind we get the default, which appears as inconsiderate and uncompromising.

3. The end of IT suffering

Like the Buddhist path to the cessation of suffering by renouncing desire and attachment, addressing poor IT service experience requires the renouncement of output-oriented service level agreements and associated metrics. Instead, the focus should be on outcome: IT's business impact and how people experience the business impact, the service interactions, and the relationship with the service provider. Experience is measured in terms of judgments and feelings, for example how quick a service interaction that took 90 objective minutes was subjectively perceived. This will differ from person to person, and for each person, from occasion to occasion, depending on a variety of factors. This makes experience so hard to 'manage'. Yet, how irrational it often appears, it is the only thing that counts. People's decisions are primarily emotional, which are then rationalized.

4. The path to the end of IT suffering

Develop an understanding of experience-dominant logic in general, explore the dynamics of the specific situation, agree and maybe formalize the desired impact of specific IT services on people and their business, and continually hypothesize and experiment to improve the IT service experience.

DEX improves when IT leadership cares enough to make changes in first acknowledging the problems, taking action to formalize the desired business impact and experience. Sometimes, particularly when the IT service is a commodity such as connectivity, the only feasible desired experience is 'good enough' - there is no point in aiming for 'delightful' connectivity. This is different when a solution is in the genesis or custom-built stage (these terms refer to Wardley mapping). In these cases, delight *is* feasible.

Buddhism teaches wisdom and compassion. In IT, an understanding of the impact of your work on people and their business, and a concern for how they think and feel, will help you make better things that make things better.

6.2 Failed IT state

IT has had a rough ride, and by extension, so have the users of IT systems. When computing technology was first introduced into organisations in the 1960s and 1970s, they were seen as expensive bean counters. Technology teams were managed by leaders who knew very little about this nascent domain. So, technology teams became used to telling business teams what could or could not be achieved. Over time, technology evolved and fragmented into specialist functional areas, and so did the myriad of use cases to which technology could be applied. Yet IT was still treated as a cost centre, and often managed by people who didn't fully understand these new technical domains. Technologists were often incentivised to over-promise (or worse, were forced into difficult situations by business leaders), which in turn led to the inevitable failure of IT investments.

Stockholm syndrome

Users (unlike IT) are regular people and regular people tend to adapt to uncomfortable situations. People need defence mechanisms in order to survive. Ever felt happy with an application when you've completed a longish transaction without it having crashed and losing your data? Yep, that's the Stockholm syndrome: "a paradoxical psychological phenomenon wherein hostages express adulation and have positive feelings towards their captors that appear irrational in light of the danger or risk endured by the victims, essentially mistaking a lack of abuse from their captors as an act of kindness". Think of some applications as benevolent dictators. You're obliged to use them and they direct your actions in a polite but firm way: "Please re-enter your data". Including the data that it could have but hasn't bothered to save for you.

The users are revolting

Back to the users. There's something in the air. The younger generations of users have completely different and irreverent opinions about IT. "IT's just there to be used." Smartphones, tablets and apps are just expected to work within the corporate IT environment. As a result of the consumerisation of technology, there's an undercurrent of discontent about the current IT regime and social media has made this painfully transparent. Even if a dictator's benevolent, he's still a dictator. Users want to be recognized as somebody who's in a relationship with an application, either out of their free volition or because their organizations require them to use it. And they want a say in the relationship. So, give them the vote. And don't fiddle with the ballot boxes – they want transparency.

Truth and reconciliation

The IT industry – albeit well-intentioned – could have done a better job at serving the business. Costs are too high and lack transparency. Although cloud services have shifted the balance of power between provider and consumer, some external vendors make it difficult to switch to alternative solutions. There are concerns about data breaches and misuse of sensitive information – not that this is purely an IT problem, but IT is a convenient scapegoat.

User organizations are frustrated as they are forced to adapt their processes to work around technical constraints rather than the other way around. Licensing agreements are difficult to understand and may lead to unexpected costs. IT overpromises the capabilities of their products or services, only for user organizations to find that the technology doesn't meet their expectations. User organizations reported frustration with slow response times, unhelpful support, and difficulty in getting technical issues resolved. The production of electronics, energy consumption of data centres, and electronic waste disposal raise concerns about sustainability and the industry's contribution to climate change. Ethical concerns have arisen regarding the use of AI and automation in IT, especially in areas like surveillance, facial recognition, and autonomous weapons.

The time has come for a Truth and Reconciliation Commission to address the alleged 'crimes against IT-humanity' committed by the IT industry. There is a desire for the expression of contrition for past sins, conviction that user organizations deserve better, and commitment to the emergence of transparency, ethics, and innovation from the ashes of these digital grievances.

6.3 IT's reputation paradox

This paragraph delves into the paradoxical nature of IT services, where being invisible can lead to underappreciation while disruptions provide an opportunity for reputation enhancement. By understanding this paradox and leveraging effective recovery strategies, IT service providers who walk this tightrope, foster more customer loyalty and trust than their technically superior competitors.

Essential but unseen

Utility services, such as water, gas, energy, and basic IT services, are often considered essential necessities. Customers rely on these services for their daily lives and expect them to be readily available and function seamlessly. When everything is running smoothly, customers may not even think about or notice these services because they are expected to be present and operational. This 'invisibility' of the service leads to a lack of appreciation of the efforts of the IT service provider.

Users are usually not particularly happy

Customers expect utility services to be reliable, accessible, and consistently available. When these expectations are met, they may not feel particularly happy because their needs are being fulfilled as anticipated. However, if the service falls short, they may become frustrated or dissatisfied. The same applied to the service agents when their own technology fails them in dealing with the technology for the end users.

IT service providers aim for the zone of tolerance

Due to the critical nature of utility services, customers are more likely to notice and remember issues or disruptions rather than extended periods of service-as-usual. When a problem occurs, this negative experience tends to overshadow the unnoticed benefits and create a perception that the service is only noticed when it fails. This suggests that IT service providers should be as invisible as possible by preventing problems. IT service providers therefore tend to aim for customer satisfaction in the zone of tolerance rather than delight.

Occasional disruptions are good for customer satisfaction

Paradoxically, IT service providers can improve their reputation when disruptions occur. And they will occur. Complex IT systems are by their very nature hazardous[15], and it is impractical to eliminate every single cause of failure. Although customer satisfaction takes an initial dip when there is an issue with the service, there is a distinct possibility that, if the issue is resolved effectively, customer satisfaction will increase. Elements of service recovery that contribute to customer satisfaction are (1) swift and effective technical recovery plus restoration of service-as-usual. (2) perceptions of honesty and fairness during the recovery process, (3) personal attention and genuine concern, and (4) plausible commitment to learning from service failures. This is often known as the service recovery paradox and dates back to the early 1990s.

Guilt-free firefighting fosters trust and loyalty

It would be unethical for firefighters to start a fire to demonstrate their value. Fortunately, from a customer satisfaction perspective, IT service providers don't need to resort to these tactics. Because we are dealing with complex and intrinsically hazardous systems, disruptions will occur from time to time. It is just the way things are. Anyone who thinks otherwise clearly has little experience with the system as found and lives in the world of the system as imagined.

---

[15] Seminal paper 'How complex systems fail' by Richard I. Cook

IT service providers that deal with these situations appropriately, can generate more trust and loyalty than competitors that are unfortunate enough to provide undisrupted service.

6.4 Both sides matter

Service experience is usually equated with customer experience but it is just as important to attend to how the provider's employees experience the service. This is not only important for their own emotional well-being, but also impacts the provider as employer, and the customer.

As an employer, the provider benefits from happier employees in terms of improved productivity and cost and effort related to management attention, retention and replacement. Happier employees also improve the reputation of the organization, making it more attractive for new employees, customers, investors and other stakeholders. The same applies to the customer, of course.

The customer benefits from happier employees in terms of their engagement and commitment. This generates a sense of trust that encourages customers to reciprocate and engage in more depth, developing the relationship.

This is explored in more detail in Appendix 2 – Is the what worth the how?

To complicate matters, in addition to their role of provider of IT services, the IT service provider's employees are also users of the IT services that support their service-providing work.

7. IT service experience management

This chapter describes how service experience is managed as an integral part of IT service management as described in Chapter 5. It offers guidance in the four areas introduced in Section 5.3.

For readers who are familiar with ITIL 4, the practical guidance in this chapter is mapped to (clusters of) relevant management practices. For a better understanding of these practices, see the ITIL 4 Practice Guides and consider the ITIL 4 Practice Manager courses and certifications. Many of these practices contain guidance related to managing IT service experience, and illustrate how it is an integral part of IT service management. Other IT service management frameworks also include references to IT service experience, some more explicitly than others. ISM 5, for example, refers explicitly to customer experience, user experience, experience indicators (XI), and service (experience) level agreements (SxLA®). Of all the IT service management frameworks, ITIL 4 offers the most detailed guidance, both in general, and regarding experience in particular. In addition to the relevant practice guides, the Drive Stakeholder Value module offers valuable guidance regarding service relationships, agreements, interactions, experience, and value. There are also two white papers referring to service experience: Experience level agreements in ITIL 4 (2019), and Elevating the IT service experience (2020), both available to ITIL subscribers/members.

As mentioned previously, experience is just one of many dimensions of IT service quality that have to be managed. Given that many people are looking for example of actions to take, this chapter makes some suggestions to consider.

The suggestions are presented in four sections based on the generic areas of IT service management:

7.1 Engagement: where agreements (XLAs) are made about the desired IT service experience and where expectations are set.
7.2 Preparation: Preparation: where the appropriate set of people and resources is selected, and where work is organized.
7.3 Co-creation: where people apply their skills and other resources, and where the outcome is measured as well as possible.
7.4 Evolution: where outcomes are analysed, improvement hypotheses are created, and experiments are conducted.

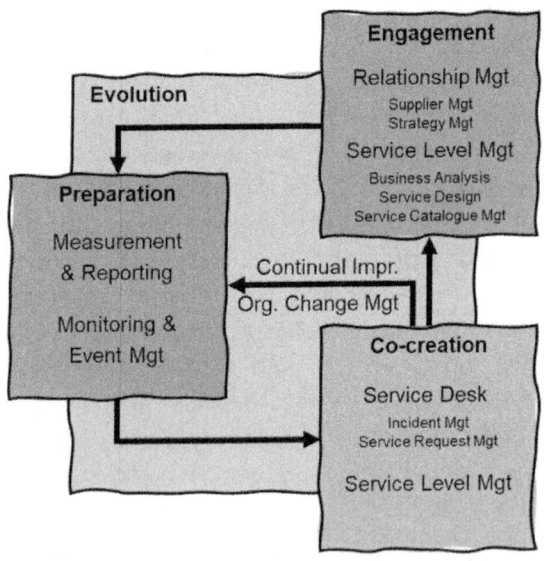

```
                    Engagement
     Evolution      Relationship Mgt
                    Supplier Mgt
                    Strategy Mgt
                    Service Level Mgt
                    Business Analysis
    Preparation     Service Design
                    Service Catalogue Mgt
    Measurement
    & Reporting     Continual Impr.
                    Org. Change Mgt
    Monitoring &
    Event Mgt       Co-creation
                    Service Desk
                    Incident Mgt
                    Service Request Mgt
                    Service Level Mgt
```

Figure: key experience-related practices/processes

Other cyclical frameworks

While the Groovy ITSM Framework is used in this book to structure IT service experience-related activities, other frameworks are equally useful, such as the two described briefly below. It is important, however, not only to understand the dynamics of the IT service experience management, but how it is embedded in regular IT service management.

Giarte's XLA® 6P Framework (the 'practice areas' part):
- Interact between consumer and provider
- Measure sentiment, performance and context
- Assess data for problem areas
- Explore the problem and possible solutions
- Agree on the best solution
- Restructure the operating model
- Refine the way of working within the operating model

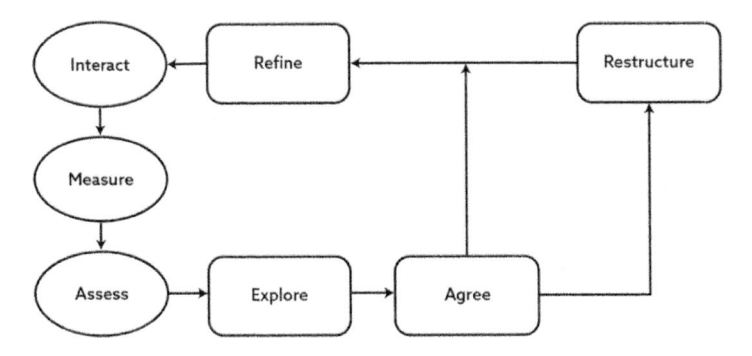

Figure: XLA practice areas[16]

HappySignals' ITXM™ Framework:

- Measure experiences
- Share the experience data
- Identify improvements
- Improve what matters most

---

[16] XLA Pocketbook by Marco Gianotten and https://giarte.com/blog/xla-pocketbook-blog-2

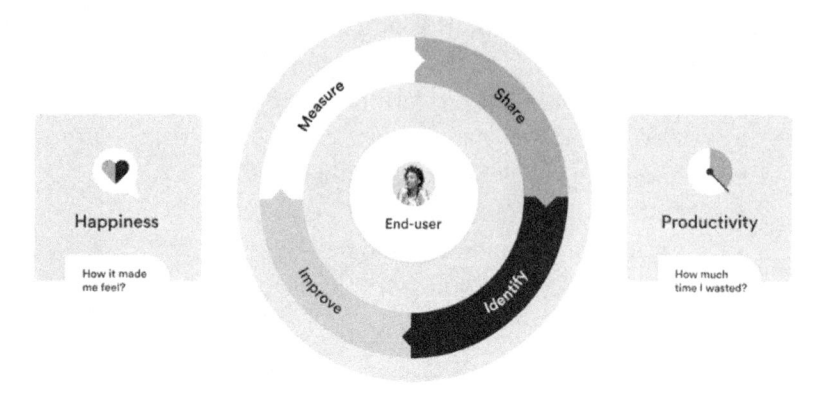

Figure: ITXM™ Framework[17]

7.1 Engagement

Engagement is where service provider and consumer discover each other's existence and assess both each other's potential contribution and potential relationship. It is not only about the initial encounter but also about the recurring assessment of the relationship and the agreement.

Stories, experiences and expectations

Parties always engage with each other based on their stories about themselves, the other party, and their relationship. These stories emerge over time, based on their experience with direct and indirect interactions. Initially, before actually meeting each other and having a direct interaction, the stories about the other party are based on touchpoints such as marketing expressions and comments by friends and strangers, all moderated by biases (or, in more neutral terms, evolutionary heuristics[18]). These stories go hand in hand with experiences and expectations: when people

---

[17] IT Experience Management Framework
https://www.happysignals.com/itxm-framework-it-experience-management
[18] Dave Snowden

deal with government agencies, they often feel fearful of being treated as a number and being passed from one anonymous department to another, and therefore manage their own case carefully so as to have evidence when things inevitably go wrong. On the other hand, when people deal with a local trader recommended by neighbours, they feel more confident and are trusting.

In time and over time

After having some direct interactions, these initial stories are refined. Experience of the relationship accrues *over time*, based on multiple *in-time* experiences of interactions (often transactions) including the outcome of the interactions.

For example, the plumber is trustworthy (relationship) because although it takes a lot of effort to arrange a visit (interaction), they are always friendly and don't make a mess (interaction), do a good job for a fair price (output), resulting in confidence that the leakage will not reoccur (outcome).

Formal agreements

IT service providers are often reluctant to commit to targets that are beyond their circle of control[19]. This is demonstrated by the prevalence of SLA targets related to technical aspects such as availability of system components. Taking a step beyond this conform zone requires a collaborative relationship with the specific customer, realistic and adaptable goal-setting, access to data to assess progress, and a reassuring risk assessment. When the provider's specific customer-related uncertainty is combined with their unfamiliarity with managing IT service experience in general, it is natural that providers want to proceed with caution. A first step towards enhancing an SLA with XLA aspects could be to

---

[19] Steven Covey popularized the Stoic philosophers' concept of the concentric circles of control, influence and concern, which help understand what is unchangeable, and what can be changed.

formalise the provider's commitment to address the impact of the IT services on people and their business, and to work towards quantifiable measurement and specific targets. This could be realized by incorporating experience and impact commitment clause as part of a new SLA, or as an appendix to an existing SLA. See Appendix 5 for an example.

PRACTICAL GUIDANCE

IT service experience management is an integral part of IT service management, and the practical guidance below is structured within two major IT service management practices and shown with a 'tick' bullet. Some other relevant practices (not explored explicitly here) are: supplier management (closely related to relationship management, but in the 'other direction'), business analysis, service design, service catalogue management.

The guidance is mainly for providers that engage with customers individually, rather than as a mass market such as served by a global cloud service provider.

Relationship management

Relationship management fosters positive connections between the organization and its stakeholders at all levels. Relationship management is also closely related to strategy management that meets stakeholders' evolving needs, so:

- ✓ Include experience as part of the strategic positioning of the organization; for example, formulate what kind of stories that the stakeholders (in particular, customers, employees and suppliers) should and should not share about the organization.

The key concept in relationship management is a model of the relationship that describes the extent of shared interests among involved parties, the progression of the service journey including potential opportunities and risks, as well as clarity regarding who does what.

Given that service experience is not only about the service interaction and its output and outcome but also the relationship:

✓ For each relationship, determine the desired experience.
✓ Study the stages of service journey with the desired experience in mind and identify opportunities and risks to improve how the relationship is experienced.
✓ Decide on the right kind of behaviour for the various actors. For examples of effective behaviour, see Appendix 4 – XLA behaviour levels.

Service level management

Service level management establishes business-oriented objectives for service performance and ensures that the delivery of services is rigorously evaluated and observed, and managed accordingly.

Given that IT service experience management is about better human experience and more business impact:

✓ Elicit the customer's underlying needs in terms of experience and impact and select or (re)design[20] appropriate services; start with the customer's business and work back through what that means for the employees, and how IT systems support them.
✓ Improve the description[21] of services in the service catalogue to help set expectations regarding experience and impact.

---

[20] For inspiration beyond the IT domain, consider Emotional Design: Why We Love (or Hate) Everyday Things by Don Norman
[21] Hank Marquis provides some examples in http://www.itsmsolutions.com/newsletters/DITYvol2iss41.htm
Such as: "Monday through Friday, from 8am to 5pm EST, when operating under normal conditions an authorized user of the system can retrieve a customer record in less than 5 seconds. No more than 10 times during the month when operating under normal conditions will any record take more than 30 seconds to retrieve."

✓ Discuss and agree principles and process-related aspects of IT service experience management, even if quantifiable measurement and specific targets are not yet feasible (see Appendix 5 – Experience and impact commitment clause).

✓ Include experience-related quality levels in the service levels offered: define the experience objectives (for example, quick service desk interaction) and the associated experience indicators (for example, objective speed and subjective speed).

✓ Include experience metrics in the service review and service quality reporting, frame these as hypotheses and best possible approximations of actual experience, discuss their perceived accuracy, and propose refinements.

7.2 Preparation

Preparation is where the agreement is translated into the people and resources ("service components") required for the actual service interactions. Although there is a grey area between preparation and evolution, preparation is mainly about working within the operating model, while evolution is mainly about improving the operating model.

A key additional aspect for IT service experience management is the setting up of the system for monitoring and measurement of experience-related facts, judgements, and feelings. This means that there are consequences for the scope of monitoring and event management, and measurement and reporting. Some other relevant practices (not explored explicitly here) are: availability management, and capacity and performance management.

PRACTICAL GUIDANCE

Monitoring and event management

Monitoring and event management involves a systematic process of continuously observing services and their constituent components. It records and reports specific changes in their status, also known as events.

Given that there can be useful correlations between objective facts and subjective judgements and feelings:

✓ Identify events that may be related to how a service is experienced, and monitor these.

Measurement and reporting

Measurement and reporting plays a crucial role in enhancing decision-making and fostering continual improvement by reducing uncertainty. This encompasses a wide spectrum, including products and services, operational practices, activities within the value chain, and all parties involved.

Given that business impact of IT services and IT service experience can be approximated by a combination of objective and subjective metrics:

✓ Start by establishing the overarching business indicators or metrics such as orders shipped, hypothesize how these are affected by IT services, and define indicators and metrics such as system availability.
✓ Define experience-related objectives and hypothesize plausible indicators for realization of the objectives; establish which metrics, data[22] and targets represent the indicators; for example:
   o Objective: quick service desk interaction
   o Indicator 1: objective speed
      ▪ Metric 1: resolution time
      ▪ Data 1: timestamps in ITSM system

---

[22] When constructing XLAs, look for experiential data sources in non-traditional places. For example, the percentage of users who request application installations within the first 72 hours after a PC refresh.

- Target 1: 80% <3 business hours and 90% <7 business hours
  - Indicator 2: subjective speed
    - Metric 2: CSAT (1-5)
    - Data 2: Answers to survey question "how quickly was your problem solved?"
    - Target 2: Average >3 and increasing

	SLA example	XLA example	XLA example	XLA example
Indicator	Objective speed	Subjective speed (judgment)	Ease (judgment)	Consideration (feeling)
Metric	Resolution time	CSAT (1-5)	CES (1-5)	CSAT (1-5)
Data	Time stamps in ITSM system	Answers to "how quickly was your problem solved?"	Answers to "how easy was it to get your problem resolved?"	Answers to "how seriously did you feel taken?"
Target	80% <3 bus. hours 90% <7 bus. hours	Average >3 and increasing	Average >2 and increasing	Average >3 and increasing

Table: possible metrics for the desired service experience of quick, easy and considerate service desk interaction

✓ Carefully consider how automated surveys are deployed to measure experience. The number and quality of the questions, and the timing and frequency of the surveys, is crucial. Poor surveys can exacerbate poor service, adding insult to injury. For more thoughts on surveys, see Appendix 6 - Surveys and alternatives.

7.3 Co-creation

Co-creation[23] is where service provider and consumer apply their knowledge, skills and other resources for mutual benefit. This is where service interactions take place and are experienced by the end users. The experience of these affordances and performances extends beyond the interaction and is also about the service interaction's output and outcome. For example, the business

---

[23] In polls conducted at events, co-creation is the consistently highest priority of area for improvement, see Appendix 7 – Changing perceptions of XLA.

impact (outcome) when someone acts on a decision that was improved by information (output) that a user derived from an application.

In addition to these primary activities between service provider and consumer, some supporting activities take place during co-creation. Monitoring and event management, and measurement and reporting (both set up in preparation – see Section 7.2) are put into practice. In addition, the relationship management model (developed in engagement – see Section 7.1) is followed. This ensures that the relationships with other stakeholders than the user and customer are monitored and developed. The practical guidance in this section focuses on the primary activities related to service desk and associated practices, and service level management.

As described in more detail in Section 6.3, end users of IT service often have a neutral experience when service is as expected. Paradoxically, the experience can improve when disruptions occur. Although the in-time experience takes an initial dip when there is an issue with a service, the over-time experience will be improved if the issue is resolved effectively.

As stated in Section 6.4 and reflected in the 'co-creation' title of this section, this is two-way traffic. Service interactions are more effective when the service recipient actively participates.

PRACTICAL GUIDANCE

Service desk

The service desk captures demand for incident resolution and service requests, and is therefore closely related to incident management and service request management. Another relevant practice (not explored explicitly here) is: capacity and performance management.

Given that the experience of IT services is strongly influenced by service desk interactions, apply empathy not only to affect both parties' emotional well-being and, in so doing, strengthen the relationship, but also to conduct more effective service interactions.

✓ As a service agent:

- o Consult available data about the situation; for example, the end user and their context, and their previous interactions, actions and results.
- o Express concern and ask an open question to elicit indications of both the human experience and the business impact; for example, "I'm sorry that this has happened – how is it affecting you?"
- o Let the end user know what is already known so that they know that they do not have to start from scratch; for example, "I see that this is the third time you have called about this issue" or "my co-worker has just briefed me about what you told her and I gather that you'd like some more detailed information about your laptop", and ask whether this interpretation is correct or needs improvement.
- o Recognize that each end user is unique, and tailor your communication style and level of technical detail accordingly; for example, some people are only concerned about the results, while others prefer to be informed and possibly involved in the resolution steps, in which case the agent could ask "do you have any thoughts about what might be causing the issue?"
- o Realize that the end user is conducting the conversation based on their experience with and expectations of the service provider, in combination with how they just happen to be feeling at the moment; for example, although the query is about a delay in providing access to non-crucial data, the end

user may bear a grudge from when the service provider treated them poorly six months ago when they were going through an unrelated personal trauma.
- o Anticipate what the user needs to know or do, based on where they are in the service journey
- o After a non-trivial issue is (deemed to be) resolved, check in with the end user to ensure everything is functioning as expected and, in so doing, to show commitment to their satisfaction beyond the immediate interaction.
- o Also consider how expectations are affected in service interactions, because people's expectations strongly influence their experience.

✓ As an end user:

- o Acknowledge that service agents are also human beings and often under stress; for example, open the conversation by asking "how is your shift going so far?"
- o Be as specific and detailed as possible when making a query; for example, describe the symptoms, error messages, and any troubleshooting steps already taken.
- o Keep in mind that service agents are often limited by policies and procedures but can help in negotiating these constraints; for example, say "I understand that you can't do this. Can we explore workarounds or could we maybe escalate this?"
- o Show appreciation for the agent's effort if they seem to have done their best.

Service level management

As described in Section 7.1 – Engagement, service level management sets clear business-oriented targets for service levels, and ensures that delivery of services is properly assessed, monitored, and managed against these targets. Service level management therefore also manifests itself in the co-creation area, where services are monitored. Section 7.2 – Preparation described how the closely-related practices monitoring and event management, and measurement and reporting were configured for collection of data regarding experience-related facts, judgements, and feelings.

In the co-creation area, customer and user satisfaction surveys are conducted and ongoing service quality is monitored according to what has been designed and set up, and service reviews and service quality reporting take place.

Both service provider and service consumer review the quality of service, usually separately but sometimes jointly. Many service providers have a formal review process that generates input for continual improvement and for service reporting. Service consumers may have a formal review process but this often informal and only triggered when there are issues with the service. Whether formalized or not, the stakeholders on both sides develop over-time experiences of the agreement and the overarching relationship.

Assuming that the stakeholders' subjective experiences influence their decisions more than objective characteristics of the services:

- ✓ Review the various sources of information about experience-related facts, judgements, and feelings about the service interactions, output, outcome, and the relationship.
- ✓ Make judgements about the hypothesized correlation between these metrics and refine the hypotheses accordingly.

✓ Provide both operational reports of the objective facts and subjective judgements and feelings, and also analytical reports that explore experience-related trends, plausible explanations, and proposals for decision-making.

✓ Jointly review the (analytical) reports and take decisions within the current agreement, or propose refinement of the agreement.

7.4 Evolution

As mentioned in Section 5.3, evolution is where the whole of engagement, preparation and co-creation is elevated to a higher level. The key topics are status (of the system) and improvements. This is therefore about understanding where you are and making changes for the better. These are the two main parts of this section.

UNDERSTANDING WHERE YOU ARE

Starting with "understanding where you are", this can vary from a situation where technically-oriented IT service management is practiced and stakeholders are dissatisfied, to where continual improvement is practiced and stakeholders are satisfied, but realize that expectations always change and therefore require continuous attention.

Effectiveness

At one end of this spectrum, IT service experience management has not yet been introduced, while at the other end, the organization's operating model[24] comprises values, competences,

---

[24] A business model describes how an enterprise creates, delivers, and captures value and sustains itself in the process, and the operating model is the 'back end' of the business model that describes the creation and delivery of value. It illustrates relationships between the elements of the organization (such as people, activities and resources) that are important for delivering the value propositions. Sources: Operating Model Canvas

processes, tools other elements that are needed to manage IT service experience.

Coverage

Not only can the effectiveness of adoption vary: the coverage of adoption across the organization can also vary. Starting with low coverage, IT service experience management can be practiced (with a certain degree of success) within one team for all of their agreed services, or even for just one of that team's services. When the coverage is high, all teams practice IT service experience management (each with its own certain degrees of success).

Areas of IT service experience management

Another variable concerns the areas of IT service experience management that are practiced. This can be mapped to the ITSM areas of engagement, preparation, co-creation, and evolution itself. IT service experience management can be executed in any of these areas. For example, on the service provider side:

- Engagement: the desired service experience is discussed, and documented in the agreement
- Preparation: the service is allocated to a team, and a system for measuring experience is designed and deployed
- Co-creation: empathy is applied to interpersonal service interactions, and experience is measured
- Evolution: hypothesized correlations between metrics and experience are evaluated, and improvement experiments are conducted

Ideally, IT service experience management is executed in each of these areas but, in practice, the current emphasis for a specific team or service might be on discussing and understanding the desired experience despite there being no mechanism to formally

---

(Campbell), Defining the IT Operating Model (Smalley, Campbell, Fulton).

measure the experience. Or vice versa, the team may be measuring the experience in preparation for discussing it with the user organization.

Influence

A key aspect of understanding where you are is understanding who you are, in that space, and how much change you can enable. Someone has a desire to improve the state of affairs and is therefore assessing their current situation and making plans for improvement. Their ability to enable change not only depends on their capabilities but also their status in the organization. In turn, their status depends on a combination of their formal authority and informal (social) prestige based on their success and virtue. In a given situation, there are things that a person can control, things that they cannot control but can influence to a degree, and things that are beyond their influence. Being effective is about understanding these differences.

Budgets

In organizational terms, a person is either 'above the line' or 'below the line'. In practical terms, they either create budgets or depend on other people's budgets to get things done. People above the line formulate policy and task people below the line to execute it.

Management factory

The traditional and seductively reassuring way of thinking about how organizations work is that managers plan and direct, and that workers comply and execute. Except that things don't work that way. At least, not effectively. The need for change often originates from the people who execute the work and are therefore most aware of its effectiveness and efficiency. Unfortunately, managers often act in a what John Seddon calls the 'management factory', where they take decisions based on what they *think* is happening in operations. Richard Cook makes a similar distinction in talking about the 'system as found' versus the 'system as imagined'. There are people who work with people, people who work with things, and people who work with information about people and things.

Decision-making

To be effective, decision-making has to be informed by operations, where the work actually takes place. There are, of course, also strategic reasons for decisions that operations is less aware of, but decision-makers should always be aware of what is actually happening in operations – if only to assess the consequences of their decisions. The alignment between decision-making and operations can be improved in various ways. Firstly, those who report to manager can improve the information that they report.

Secondly, managers can directly observe what happens in operations; in Lean thinking this is called 'going to Genba[25]'. Finally, managers can delegate (some) decision-making to operations.

Intelligent disobedience

Intelligent disobedience is when a service animal trained to help a disabled person goes directly against the owner's instructions in an effort to make a better decision. It can also be applied to organizations. When a worker is confronted with a situation that, based on the organization's mission or on defensible ethics, requires action that deviates from policies or processes, they should do the right thing. In the healthier kind of organizations, managers acknowledge their fallibility and foster psychologically safe environments where people can take such actions without fear for their reputation or position. In preparation of making improvements, it is also good to understand how intelligently disobedient an organization is.

---

[25] Japanese for actual place – where the work happens; also spelled as Gemba

Summary

The first step in evolution is understanding where you are and who you are. This is about understanding how IT service experience management is practiced, how decisions are taken, and how much influence the aspiring change maker has.

MAKING CHANGES FOR THE BETTER

Kaizen

While recognizing that what works well in one culture will probably work differently in another culture, the Japanese Kaizen principle is worth consideration. It means, broadly speaking, continuous improvement. 'Kai' means 'change' and 'zen' means 'for the better'.

Its application can humanize the workplace, empowering individual members to identify areas for improvement and suggest practical solutions. Kaizen comprises many elements such as Genba walks, value stream mapping and quality circles, but the most fundamental step is fostering a culture of continuous improvement where every employee is encouraged to suggest and implement improvements regularly. Once this has been established, improvements will start to emerge.

Adoption stages

Organizations go through various stages when adopting XLA and adapting it to whatever works for them. Here are some aspects that could help them assess where they are.

Culture	Agreements	Measurements	Interactions
Technical People focus on technology and processes, rather than human experience or business impact	**Technical** SLAs refer to IT system components and processes	**Technical** Events and status regarding IT system components and processes are measured objectively	**Transactional** Interactions are technical and transactional, with little interest for the outcome and relationship
Recognition Some people understand how IT services affect people and their business, but the need for change is not widely recognized	**Informal** XLA has been discussed with the user organization, and there are vague expectations	**Basic** Some aspects of subjective human experience and business impact are measured, probably using existing ITSM tools	**Recognition** Some people recognize the human and business significance of interactions, and make individual improvements
Local A team has developed its own XLA principles, either as a formal pilot or under corporate radar	**Process** SLAs have been extended with an improvement process, but omit experience and impact levels	**Comprehensive** A coherent set of experience and impact metrics is measured, enabled by specialized DEM tools	**Empathy** Interactions are empathic but not always translated into concrete results
Emerging More teams are developing, sharing, and adopting XLA principles	**Experience** SLAs have been extended with desired human experience levels	**Correlated** Experience and impact metrics are correlated with technical metrics	**Compassion** Interactions are both empathic and effective
Integrated Most teams have embraced common XLA principles, and it is part of the organization's identity	**Impact** SLAs have been extended with desired business impact levels	**Predictive** Analytics and predictive models help anticipate potential issues and pro-actively optimize	**Relational** The relationship is leading in the interactions, and realistic expectations are set

The five stages of the four aspects do not have distinct boundaries but characterize their approximate position on a development continuum.

Roles

As described in the section Influence earlier in this chapter, people who aspire to enable change have varying degrees of influence. Here is a plausible categorization of roles:

- Directors create budgets and direct managers to execute improvement initiatives.
- Managers task consultants to design and realize improvements.
- Consultants advise managers, and coordinate and execute improvements.
- Workers adopt sensible ideas and refine them to make them work in practice. They pay lip service to the rest.
- Guerrillas[26] have other plans and initiate improvements under corporate radar, with or without implicit managerial approval.

Directors and managers, advised and supported by consultants, can change the operating model (for example, policies, processes, roles, competences, teams, tools, contracts), while workers and guerrillas can only make changes within the constraints of the operating model.

In the context of IT service experience management, directors and managers and their consultants will typically consider improvement initiatives such as:

- Launch a corporate awareness programme around quality of service, service experience, customer experience, employee experience, etc.
- Create a temporary task force or permanent experience management office (XMO) to initiate, facilitate and coordinate IT service experience management activities in the various IT service teams
- Train employees in understanding IT service experience and practicing its management

---

[26] People who act in an impromptu way, often without authorization. People who work in an organization that does not embrace the triple bottom line of people, planet and profit, will probably have to resort to guerrilla tactics to create pockets of care and consideration.

Workers will tend to make improvements such as:

- Discuss and understand the desired experience during the agreement process, even if it does not get formalized in the agreement document
- Incorporate experience-related indicators in the SLA, without explicitly mentioning XLA
- Pay more attention to how users express themselves in service interactions, and acknowledge and respond to their emotions

Guerrillas will add to the workers' initiatives; for example:

- Find like-minded individuals or a small team of passionate advocates who understand the 'mission' and are willing to work behind the scenes to drive improvements
- Collect data on user experiences, pain points, and areas that need improvement, and keep records of improvements as evidence of success when seeking official recognition
- Align initiatives – even just cosmetically – with supportive official policies and strategies, such as corporate programmes for customer satisfaction

PRACTICAL GUIDANCE

The guidance in this section primarily maps to two ITIL 4 practices that are so closely-related that a distinction between the two is not made in the guidance provided. The two main practices are continual improvement and organizational change management. Some other relevant practices (not explored explicitly here) are: business analysis, portfolio management and strategy management.

Continual improvement and organizational change management

Continual improvement involves the consistent alignment of an organization's practices and services with evolving business requirements. Organizational change management, on the other hand, focuses on ensuring that changes within an organization are introduced smoothly and effectively, with due attention to human aspects.

Guidance

The "understand where you are" assessment will identify the current status of the organization and therefore help determine which steps need to be taken.

- ✓ Establish the case for change to justify the investment, for example as an 'elevator pitch':
    - o People desire emotional well-being
    - o IT service affects people and their business
    - o IT service often falls short
    - o XLA can improve IT service and its impact
    - o The IT industry has much to answer for
    - o People deserve better
    - o We feel morally obliged to act.
- ✓ Share the case for change with stakeholders to get their buy-in; note that this is both rational (benefits for service users, service agents, employers) and emotional (moral obligation, aspiration, status); the following steps assume approval of the case and allocation of budget.
- ✓ Form a small task force to drive the initiative; comprising at least a manager as a facilitator for the consultant, and a consultant to lead the improvement and coach team members.
- ✓ Select a team or a service for a pilot; preferably a team/service that will encourage interest from others.
- ✓ Train the team members to understand at least the why and the what of IT service experience management.
- ✓ Ask the front-line for their assessment of the situation.
- ✓ Actively involve the user organization in the initiative – co-creation is one of the underlying principles.

- ✓ From the start, foster a culture of continual improvement; draw inspiration from Kaizen.
- ✓ Explore the current situation and jointly decide on the areas that most require improvement (see Sections 6.1 – 6.3), and the experiments[27] to be conducted (framing the improvements as experiments is not only more realistic but also lowers the bar for commitment).
- ✓ Realize that industry guidance is imperfect and should be interpreted as 'this might work for you' – it should always be assessed against the specific circumstances, and adapted where appropriate.
- ✓ Discuss the differing degrees of complexity and therefore inherent unpredictability of the various areas of work and determine improvement approaches accordingly; draw inspiration from Cynefin.
- ✓ Encourage team members to adopt news ways of thinking and to reassess their natural reaction of applying more of what they are familiar with (for example, more technical KPIs).
- ✓ Respond to the inevitable resistance to change with understanding for the uncertainty and effort involved (for techniques to help people change.
- ✓ Appeal to the emotional dimension of the impact of IT service and the moral imperative that people deserve better
- ✓ Foster an identity ("people like us do things like this") that invites people to enrol.
- ✓ Measure progress in terms of "more stories like these and fewer stories like those"[28].
- ✓ Share how the pilot has impacted people and their business, recognising contributors who have embraced the change.
- ✓ Document the approach for use in other teams.
- ✓ Depending on the results of the pilot, either repeat the pilot with a different approach or start with broader adoption.

---

[27] Toyota Kata is useful in fostering continuous improvement based on scientific thinking

[28] Dave Snowden suggest this indicator because it is not easy to 'game'

- ✓ Integrate the new way of working into policies, procedures, and employee training, ensuring that it becomes ingrained in the organization's culture.
- ✓ Realize that circumstance change over time as a result of internal and external actions, and approaches that worked in the past might not work now, and vice versa.
- ✓ Continue to foster a culture of continual improvement (otherwise any benefit will only have been temporary).
- ✓ Discover and share ideas with other organizations at conferences and other communities.

Epilogue

Act 4: "The Valued Partner Emerges"

Characters:

- IT service manager (SM)
- Business manager (BM)

[Scene 5 - The IT Service Manager and Business Manager are having a conversation in the office. The atmosphere is positive, and they seem relieved.]

SM: (Grinning) You know, it's been quite a journey, but I'm proud of how our IT department has transformed.

BM: (Appreciative) Absolutely! The change is palpable. Our department's productivity has improved, and employees are happier.

SM: (Reflecting) It wouldn't have been possible without your support and understanding, especially when there was some resistance to new ways of working.

BM: (Grateful) Well, technology alone doesn't make a department successful. It's about the partnership and the people behind it.

[They both nod in agreement, symbolizing a strong partnership between the IT department and the business department. As they do, the lights gradually dim, and the stage curtain slowly descends, signalling the end of the play.]

Appendices

This section comprises additional elaboration on various topics that have been mentioned in the book. The appendices are referenced at appropriate parts in the relevant chapters. They are not intended to be read in the sequence below or as a coherent whole.

Some pieces have been published as separate articles on LinkedIn; these include a reference to the publication date. There is some duplication so that they make sense as individual pieces. There is also some inconsistency in terminology due to new insights, but the older insights remain valid – they are all ways of looking at a topic.

A.1 A stack of IT system components

A.2 An atlas of negative IT service emotions

A.3 Is the what worth the how?

A.4 XLA behaviour levels

A.5 Experience and impact commitment clause

A.6 Surveys and alternatives

A.7 Changing perceptions of XLA

A.8 Other XLA publications

A.1 A stack of IT system components
Published on LinkedIn in July 2023

This terse appendix is a taxonomy of components that provide an organization with digitized information. Other interpretations are available and valid. It describes a stack of artefacts, value streams, organizations, and capabilities, all related to digitized information. The first occurrence of each key term is highlighted in bold text.

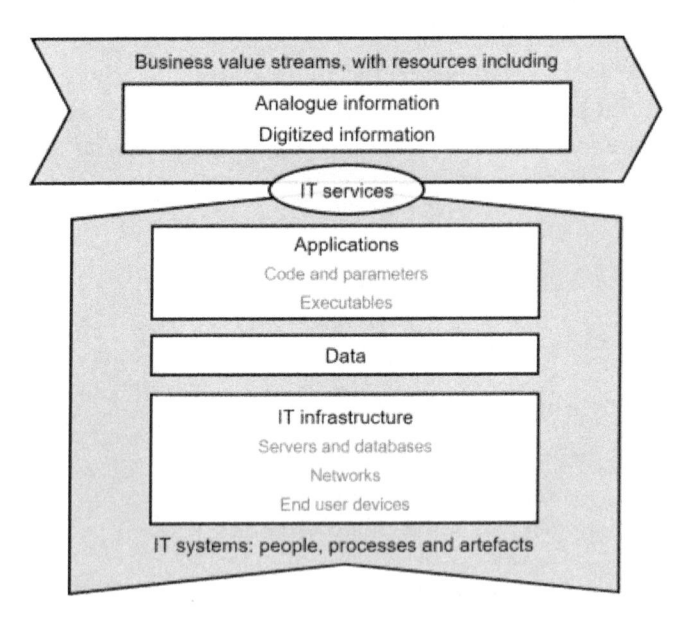

```
Business value streams, with resources including
    Analogue information
    Digitized information

        IT services

        Applications
        Code and parameters
        Executables

        Data

        IT infrastructure
        Servers and databases
        Networks
        End user devices
    IT systems: people, processes and artefacts
```

Information is one of the **resources** that **organizations** use to achieve their **objectives**. Other resources are: financial resources, people (in service science[29] referred to as operant resources that act upon operand resources), physical resources (for example, buildings, machines and technology), intangible resources (for example, software and other algorithms, intellectual property, brand reputation).

---

[29] Jim Spohrer, Wikipedia

The importance of information (**data** that is relevant for a particular context) and the capability to process data, varies from organization to organization. Data and **data processing** (collect, compute, store, transport, disseminate), and information and **information processing**, are often important enough to require **management** and, when strategically important, also **governance**.

Organizations use information as a resource that supports **operations** and its management. Some organizations use data processing as an external service (for example, bookkeeping). Some organizations use information an external service (for example, weather forecasting).

Most organizations use **digitized information** as well as **analogue (non-digitized) information**. *Digitalization* (or digital transformation) refers to the organizational and technological change to enable an organization to use **digitized data processing** to do things significantly differently, or to do significantly different things, compared to when they had less-extensively digitized data processing.

The **information system** that is needed for digitized data processing comprises technological and organizational components:

1. IT system

- **Application software**: executables that run on IT infrastructure and interact with databases; and the code and parameters that dictate their behaviour
- **Data**, stored and organized in **databases**
- **IT infrastructure**: **servers** and **end user devices**, and **networks** that connect them, each comprising **software**, data and **hardware**

2. **Organization**: people who execute and manage the required activities, and are organized in a chain or network of **parties**, primarily

- **User organizations** that decide what information and data processing is required to support their activities; engage with an IT service provider to make agreements about the acquisition of IT services that afford users access to the appropriate IT systems, and perform activities that support the user organization in their IT-related **needs**; use IT services and IT systems to fulfil those needs
- **Leading IT service providers** that engage with the user organization to make agreements about the provision of appropriate IT services; engage with other IT service providers, and IT product providers to make agreements about IT services and IT products that are used as components of IT systems; develop and acquire IT products and IT services, and integrate them to form IT systems; allocate and arrange knowledge, skills and other resources that are needed to provide IT services; run and afford users access to the IT system, and support them in their IT needs
- **Supporting IT service providers** that provide other IT service providers with the standard or bespoke IT services that are integrated in an IT system
- **IT product providers** that provide IT service providers with IT products that are integrated in an IT service

3. **Value streams** of activities that the parties execute, that, together, achieve **value** from digitized data

- Needs to requirements
- **Requirements** to systems and services
- Systems to information: affordance of use of systems; use of systems; support of use of systems; selection and interpretation of data

- Information to value: processes use digitized data processing to save time and money (efficiency); people use information to improve decisions and then act on them (effectiveness)

4. Resources that support people and processes

5. **Management systems** that set goals, plan, organize, direct and guide, and monitor and evaluate **performance** and **improvement**.

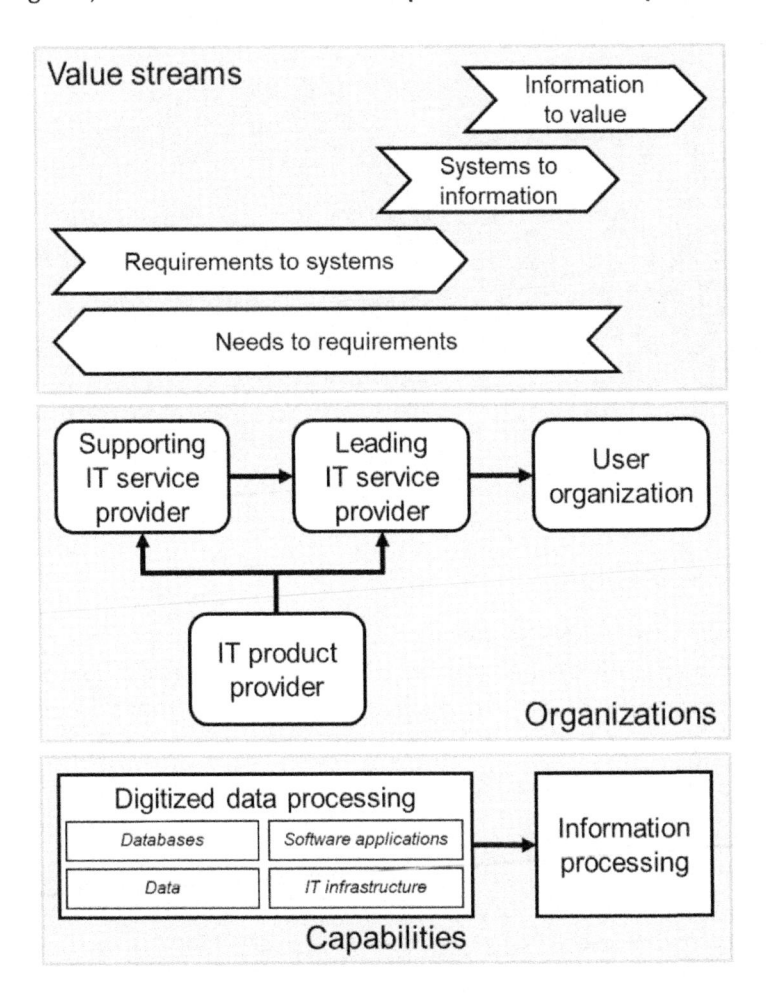

Value streams
- Information to value
- Systems to information
- Requirements to systems
- Needs to requirements

Organizations
- Supporting IT service provider → Leading IT service provider → User organization
- IT product provider

Capabilities
- Digitized data processing
  - Databases
  - Software applications
  - Data
  - IT infrastructure
- Information processing

A.2 Is the what worth the how?
Published on LinkedIn in June 2022

Here we go again. Yet another attempt to nail the nature of service and how it affects the various players involved. This new doodle introduces the distinction between principal and agent[30], where the principal has appointed an agent to act on their behalf. In my use of the terms, the principals are primarily concerned with achieving desired goals, while the agents are more concerned with the actual work.

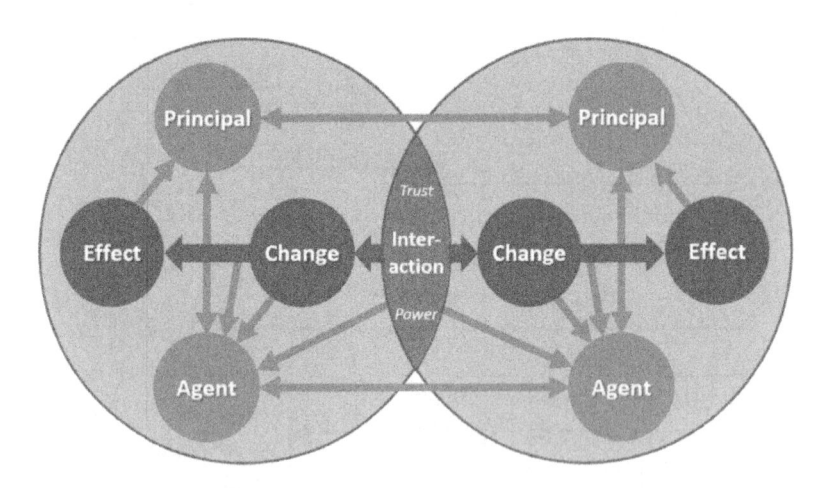

Economic exchange

The two large circles in the illustration represent organizations that engage in economic exchange by means of service. Service could also involve the exchange of ownership of goods (often called products), but that is not relevant for this exploration.

---

[30] I started thinking more about principals and agents after reading Majid Iqbal's labour of love Thinking in Services: Encoding and Expressing Strategy through Design

We tend to think in terms of a customer that pays for a supplier's services but other stakeholders are service providers or service consumers, for example a regulatory body that affords an organization the right to do business.

Note that organizations usually have multiple roles: a consumer will often be a provider for another consumer. These relationships could be depicted in a sequential chain but a network would be a better representation. The illustration above can be regarded as a window that focuses on a single relationship in the larger chain or network.

Service relationships

Two or more organizations (or service systems as they are known in service science) interact by applying their resources such as knowledge and skills for mutual benefit. The interaction occurs within the context of a relationship that is characterized in terms of trust and power.

As I wrote in Elevating the IT service experience (Axelos, 2020), trust is based on the trustor's perception of the trustee's integrity, benevolence and 'technical' abilities in relevant domains. Integrity is the adherence to acceptable principles such as honesty, openness, reliability and consistency, while benevolence is about doing good beyond what is generally expected. Trust is also based on the demonstration of the trustee's reciprocal trust and vulnerability by taking risks with behaviour outside their direct control. Trust is more than a judgement about how well the other party will perform, it is also about how effective the collaboration will be.

The balance of power also affects the relationship: for example, whether it is a buyer's or a seller's market or whether either party feels constrained by a contract.

Service interactions

Interactions result in change to each organization. The primary change will be to the organization's resources but other elements of the organization will also change, for example the trust in the other party and the knowledge and skills for better future interactions. Financial resources will also change in value. In some cases, the change will have direct effect to the principal's desired goals but in other cases the resources will have to be used in order to achieve the goals. For example, when the service is access to an information system, the agent will have to use the system in order to derive useful information. 'Change and effect' could also be seen as 'output and outcome'.

Stakeholder experience

The orange arrows indicate how the players are affected. The agents experience the interaction itself, the changes to the resources that the agents use, and the use of the changed resources in achieving the desired goals. The agents will also be affected by their counterparts' experience. The agents may not be directly affected by the contribution of their work to desired goals but will typically be affected by how the principal experiences the contribution. The principals are mainly interested in the contribution of the service and the agents' work to desired goals but they will also be affected by both their agents' experience and their counterparts' experience. These are all areas to be aware of when assessing and improving stakeholder experience.

We often distinguish between customer experience and employee experience but these are intertwined: the stakeholder experience - whether as a consumer or a provider - will always be part of their experience as an employee. Employment is also a service, involving employer and employee as the two main parties, and represented in the illustration as the relationship between principal and agent.

Value from service is always uniquely and phenomenologically determined by the beneficiary. Each individual experiences the service differently, and for each individual, the experience will differ from time to time, depending on an unpredictable combination of many factors. In the end, it is about feeling whether the what was worth the how and, if not, whether there is enough belief in improvement.

Service improvement

For people who want to start improving the quality of service by focusing on experience, the best advice is to pay attention to these areas and discuss them. Metrics may follow but that should not be the primary concern. Metrics can be based on people's reported experience and/or actual behaviour that is assumed to reflect their experience. Neither kind of metric is necessarily a good proxy for the actual experience. So, experience can be quantified with varying degrees of usefulness but it can always be qualitatively discussed. It is good to realize that the discussion itself (independent of what is discussed) is also part of the service experience, contributing to trust in the relationship.

A.3 An atlas of negative IT service emotions
Published on LinkedIn in June 2023

**Inconvenience
Impatience Annoyance
Disappointment Frustration
Helplessness Anxiety Stress
Anger Distrust Resentment**

Figure: examples of negative emotions related to service

Well, not exactly an atlas of the caliber of Eckman's Atlas of Emotions, let alone one supported by the Dalai Lama, although I am sure His Holiness would approve of any attempt to reduce IT service suffering. This is an attempt to chart the kinds of negative emotions that users encounter on an all too regular basis. The emotions are listed in approximate order of increasing severity.

Inconvenience: IT service issues can disrupt users' workflow and daily routines, causing inconvenience. This may involve system crashes, slow response times, or the need to repeat tasks due to errors, leading to annoyance and inefficiency.

Impatience: When users encounter delays or long waiting times for IT support or resolution of their issues, they may feel impatient. This can be exacerbated when urgent tasks or deadlines are at stake.

Annoyance: Users who rely on IT services to streamline their work may feel annoyed by reduced efficiency caused by poor service. This can lead to lower productivity and a sense of wasted time and effort.

Disappointment: Users may feel disappointed when it fails to meet their expectations and needs. They may have anticipated certain features, functionality, or performance, but when the service falls short, it can result in a sense of letdown.

Frustration: Users may feel frustrated when they encounter technical issues repeatedly or when they face difficulties in getting the desired results from the IT service.

Helplessness: When users encounter ongoing issues with IT service and their attempts to resolve them are ineffective, they may feel helpless. The inability to find a solution or receive adequate support can lead to a sense of powerlessness.

Anxiety: Users relying on IT services for critical tasks may experience anxiety when the service fails or performs poorly. They may worry about meeting deadlines, losing data, or facing negative consequences as a result of the IT service's shortcomings.

Stress: Problems with IT service can contribute to increased stress levels, especially if it disrupts work or personal activities. Users may experience heightened pressure to find workarounds or deal with the consequences of the service's inadequacies.

Anger: Poor IT service can also lead to anger, especially if it causes significant disruptions, loss of productivity, or financial loss. Users may feel let down by the service provider and become angry at the inconvenience caused.

Distrust: Users who repeatedly face issues may develop a sense of distrust towards the service provider. They may question the reliability and competence of the provider, which can impact their future interactions and expectations.

Resentment: Prolonged exposure to poor IT service can lead to feelings of resentment. Users may feel resentful towards the service provider for not delivering on promises, causing inconvenience, or wasting their time and resources.

A.4 XLA behaviour levels

Published on LinkedIn in June 2023

Effective IT service behaviour patterns

Summary of 21 workshops in GBR[1a], IRL, FIN, NOR, SLK, BEL, POL, AUS, JAP, AUT, NLD[2a], CAN, LVA, GER, SWE, RUS (2015-2018)

Desired behavior of IT service consumers
- Ask for outcomes, not solutions
- Articulate strategy and needs clearly, and keep the service provider updated
- Engage and participate with the service provider
- Determine risk appetite and priorities, take decisions
- Understand service provider's limitations
- Own organizational change
- Give feedback about use
- Invest in digital skills

Desired behavior of IT service providers
- Be accessible, quick, flexible, communicative and empathetic
- Engage with the service consumers and follow a common goal
- Understand the impact for both parties
- Talk benefits, costs and risks
- Discuss consequences
- Suggest innovations
- Say "Yes, if", not "No"

Figure: summary of desired behaviour from IT service consumers and providers

A few years ago, I conducted 21 workshop in 16 countries to establish effective behaviour patterns in the context of IT service. In each workshop (with on average about 20 people), the participants split themselves into two groups: IT service consumers (aka "the business") and IT service providers ("IT"). Each group discussed the kind of behaviour they would like the other party to exhibit. Then they presented their findings to each other and discussed them. I summarized the findings and updated my high-level consolidated findings (see illustration above).

At the time, I was hardly aware of the emerging Experience Level Agreement (XLA) movement that extends the scope of the Service Level Agreement (SLA) to address both the human experience and the business impact of the IT service. I certainly had not made the connection. In hindsight, however, these workshop findings can easily be seen as input for service levels for behaviour-related experience. Other XLA service levels are about the experience of the relationship in general, the business impact that the service enables, and how the business impact is experienced.

Here are examples of how these behaviour-related aspects could be included in an SLA/XLA.

Accessibility and responsiveness: IT service providers should be accessible, respond promptly to inquiries, and acknowledge service requests within a defined timeframe.

- Service level: Respond to service requests or inquiries within a specified time frame (for example, 4 business hours) and provide an initial acknowledgment.

Alignment with common goals: IT service providers should align their actions and decisions with the common goals agreed upon with the service consumers.

- Service level: Demonstrate alignment with agreed common goals through regular progress reports and updates.

Understanding the impact: IT service providers should understand the impact of their services on the service consumers' business processes and operations.

- Service level: Conduct impact assessments for major changes or incidents and communicate the results to the service consumers within a specified timeframe.

Discussion of benefits, costs, and risks: IT service providers should engage in discussions with service consumers about the benefits, costs, and risks associated with proposed IT initiatives or changes.

- Service level: Provide detailed discussions on benefits, costs, and risks for at least 50% of proposed IT initiatives.

Consequences discussion: IT service providers should discuss potential consequences, both positive and negative, of implementing or not implementing specific IT initiatives.

- Service level: Include a discussion of consequences in at least 50% of decision-making processes.

Suggesting innovations: IT service providers should actively suggest innovative solutions or improvements that can enhance the service consumers' operations.

- Service level: Present a minimum number of innovative suggestions per quarter based on industry best practices or emerging technologies.

"Yes, if" approach: IT service providers should strive to find solutions rather than simply rejecting requests. They should use a "Yes, if" approach that explores alternatives and compromises.

- Service level: Respond to service requests with a "Yes, if" approach, proposing alternative options or compromises in at least 80% of cases.

Service is about the co-creation of value by the application of knowledge, skills and other resources by both parties, where the service consumer plays an active role. So, agreements within more enlightened and emancipated relationships also include service levels for IT service consumers, such as the following examples.

Outcome-based requests: IT service consumers should provide clear outcomes they want to achieve rather than prescribing specific solutions.

- Service level: Specify at least 50% of requests in terms of outcomes rather than solutions.

Clear articulation of strategy and needs: Service consumers should clearly communicate their strategic objectives, needs, and changes in business requirements to the IT service provider.

- Service level: Maintain an updated strategy and needs document, and communicate changes within a defined timeframe.

Active engagement and participation: Service consumers should actively engage and collaborate with the IT service provider throughout the service delivery process.

- Service level: Attend scheduled meetings, provide required information, and actively participate in discussions at least 50% of the time.

Risk appetite and prioritization: Service consumers should assess their risk appetite and prioritize IT initiatives accordingly.

- Service level: Determine risk appetite and prioritize IT initiatives based on business impact within a specified timeframe.

Understanding service provider's limitations: Service consumers should acknowledge and understand the limitations of the IT service provider, such as resource constraints or technical capabilities.

- Service level: Demonstrate understanding of at least 50% of the service provider's limitations through documented discussions.

Ownership of organizational change: Service consumers should take ownership of organizational changes resulting from IT initiatives, including change management processes and end-user training.

- Service level: Develop and execute change management plans for major IT initiatives, including communication and training activities.

Feedback on service use: Service consumers should provide feedback on the use and effectiveness of IT services to facilitate continual improvement.

- Service level: Submit feedback or improvement suggestions for at least 50% of IT services used within a specified timeframe.

Investment in digital skills: Service consumers should invest in developing digital skills within their organization to leverage IT services effectively.

- Service level: Allocate a specified budget and resources for digital skills development programs and training.

These examples are based on my workshop findings. The proposed approach for a specific agreement is to conduct such a workshop with the major stakeholders (2 hours should be long enough to gather the raw input), and translate these findings into formal or informal agreements. The workshop process will probably prove to be just as valuable - if not more so - as the workshop findings and resulting service levels.

A.5 Experience and impact commitment clause

This is an example of a first formal step towards enhancing an SLA with XLA aspects. It formalizes the provider's commitment to address the impact of the IT services on people and their business, and to work towards quantifiable measurement and specific targets. The clause could be incorporated as an integral part of a new SLA or added as an appendix to an existing SLA.

Experience and impact commitment clause

Recognizing the importance of [customer]'s ("Customer") employees' subjective experience of [service provider]'s ("Provider") IT services and their potential impact on Customer's business processes and outcomes, Provider acknowledges its commitment to continually enhance and optimize the quality of their IT services. While there are currently no quantifiable metrics or specific targets in place, both parties agree to the following principles:

1. Feedback integration:
    o Provider solicits Customer's feedback and provides a communication channel for unsolicited feedback.
2. Regular assessment:
    o Provider periodically reviews and assesses the impact of the services on Customer's employees and their work.
3. Proactive improvement:
    o Provider continually seeks ways to enhance the user experience and minimize any disruptions to Customer's business processes resulting from the services, based on feedback from Customer and their own observations.

- Provider maintains open and transparent communication about their improvement efforts.
4. Future target setting:
   - As the partnership evolves and Provider gains a deeper understanding of Customer's specific needs, Provider will explore setting measurable targets for user experience and business impact, with Customer's input and agreement.

This clause underscores Provider's commitment to improving the experience and impact of the services, even in the absence of initial quantifiable metrics.

As an active participant in the co-creation of value from IT services,
   - Customer responds to requests for feedback and proactively shares insights on how the services impact their employees and their work the specific agreement, and the relationship in general.

As the partnership matures, Provider looks forward to collaboratively establishing concrete targets to align with Customer's business goals.

A.6 Surveys and alternatives

Customers are more likely to experience customer satisfaction surveys as positive when several key factors are considered and implemented by the companies conducting the surveys. Here are some factors that contribute to a positive customer satisfaction survey experience:

Timeliness: Surveys should be sent at an appropriate time after the customer has had an interaction with the company, product, or service. Sending surveys immediately after the interaction or purchase can yield more accurate and detailed feedback.

Relevance: Surveys should be relevant to the customer's experience. Tailor the questions to the specific interaction or transaction, so customers feel that their feedback is meaningful.

Brevity: Keep surveys concise and easy to complete. Long and complicated surveys can be frustrating and deter participation.

Clear purpose: Clearly communicate the purpose of the survey and how the feedback will be used. Customers are more likely to participate if they understand the value of their input.

Anonymity: Assure customers that their responses will be kept confidential. This encourages honest and candid feedback.

User-friendly interface: Ensure that the survey is accessible and easy to complete on various devices (desktop, mobile, etc.). A user-friendly interface improves the overall experience.

Follow-up: Show that you value customer feedback by acknowledging their responses and, if applicable, sharing how you plan to address their concerns or suggestions.

Personalization: Address customers by their names and personalize the survey based on their past interactions or preferences when possible. This shows that you value their individual experiences.

Closed-ended and open-ended questions: Use a mix of closed-ended (multiple-choice) and open-ended questions. Closed-ended questions provide quantitative data, while open-ended questions allow customers to express themselves in their own words.

Transparency: Be transparent about the survey results and any actions taken based on customer feedback. This demonstrates that you are committed to improving based on customer input.

Accessibility: Ensure that the survey is accessible to all customers, including those with disabilities. Compliance with accessibility standards is not only ethical but also legally required in many regions.

Testing and piloting: Test the survey with a small group of customers before launching it widely to identify any issues with question clarity, technical glitches, or overall user experience.

Frequency: Don't bombard customers with surveys. Be mindful of how often you request their feedback to avoid survey fatigue.

Responsive action: Act on the feedback received. Show customers that their input is making a difference by making improvements and addressing concerns raised in the surveys.

Ultimately, a positive customer satisfaction survey experience hinges on demonstrating that you genuinely care about your customers' opinions, making it easy for them to provide feedback, and using that feedback to enhance their experience with your company or services.

While surveys are a common and effective method for measuring customer satisfaction and identifying improvement areas, there are several alternative approaches and techniques to consider:

Customer interviews: Conduct one-on-one or group interviews with customers to gather in-depth qualitative feedback. This allows for more detailed insights and the opportunity to ask follow-up questions. It's especially useful for understanding complex issues or uncovering hidden problems.

Focus groups: Bring together a small group of customers to discuss their experiences, perceptions, and suggestions. This approach encourages open dialogue among participants and can provide valuable insights into common themes.

Customer support and service data: Analyse data from customer support interactions, including emails, chat logs, and call recordings. This can reveal common issues and pain points that customers are experiencing.

Customer complaints and feedback forms: Encourage customers to submit complaints or feedback directly through your website or customer service channels. Analysing this data can help identify recurring issues.

Customer feedback software: Implement feedback tools and widgets on your website or within your product to collect real-time feedback. This can be less intrusive than traditional surveys and capture immediate responses.

Mystery shopping: Use trained individuals or companies to act as customers and evaluate your services. This can provide an objective perspective on the customer experience.

Competitor analysis: Compare your services with those of your competitors. Identify areas where you may be falling short in terms of customer satisfaction or features.

Usability testing: Evaluate the user-friendliness of your services by observing how real customers interact with them. This can highlight areas for improvement in design and functionality.

Customer journey mapping: Map out the entire customer journey, from initial awareness to post-purchase support. This visual representation can help identify pain points and areas where improvements can be made.

Online analytics: Analyse website and app analytics to track user behaviour and identify areas where customers are dropping off or encountering issues.

Employee feedback: Employees who interact with customers regularly often have valuable insights into customer satisfaction and pain points. Conduct internal surveys or focus groups with staff.

Customer advisory boards: Create a board of loyal customers who provide ongoing feedback and insights. This group can help shape your company's strategies and product development.

Customer churn analysis: Examine the reasons why customers leave your company and seek patterns or trends that can inform improvement efforts.

The most effective approach may involve a combination of these methods, tailored to your specific industry and customer base. The key is to continuously gather feedback, analyse data, and take action to improve the customer experience based on the insights you gain. Most of this is equally applicable to users as internal 'customers' for the IT function.

A.7 Changing perceptions of XLA
Published on LinkedIn in February 2022

Highest priority / Group	Envision NL 21	Wakaru FI 21	SBA Tor CA 21	eSMF SE 21	RockMedia SE 21	SMFS CH 21	Serv.Space AT 21	Ext.serv.prov Int'l 21	SDI Int'l 22
Valuable investments	23%	8%	7%	22%	8%	10%	13%	0%	12%
Fast development	33%	32%	27%	22%	17%	25%	33%	42%	13%
Resilient operations	12%	6%	27%	11%	25%	19%	15%	7%	29%
Co-created value	20%	27%	33%	33%	42%	25%	26%	44%	34%
Assured conformance	4%	1%	0%	0%	0%	2%	0%	1%	-
Efficiency of the solutions	8%	26%	7%	11%	8%	19%	13%	13%	18%

Figure: highest priority improvement areas, based on polls at events

I had a short speaking slot at The Service Desk Institute (SDI)'s recent virtual event Changing Perceptions of IT: XLAs not SLAs and also attached the other seven presentations.

It was interesting to see how much interest there was for the topic of service experience, which correlated with the highest priority given to 'co-creation of value', which is where the rubber hits the road and the consumer actually realises the return on investment (see poll results above). In another poll, 67% of the respondents said it would take a significant change to their IT operating model to realise the desired improvement, as opposed to incremental changes to their way of working.

It was equally interesting – based on the speakers' differing perspectives – how much the field is still under construction. Not only 'Changing Perceptions of IT' but also 'Changing Perceptions of XLA'. My own understanding is also still on the move, for example in the following areas...

Experience in utility and warranty

Where I initially thought of experience as a distinct category alongside the classic utility (fitness for purpose) and warranty (fitness for use), I now see experience overlapping utility and warranty.

There is experience related to utility and experience related to warranty: I am delighted that the functionality (utility) eases my workload but annoyed how long the application takes to load (warranty).

Transient and cumulative experience

Alongside this transient experience, which occurs during the service interaction, there is also a more permanent cumulative experience, which, in turn, modulates each transient experience: the apprehension that something will probably go wrong again, detracts from what might turn out to be a faultless service. Anticipated future experience also plays a role: is it a one-night stand or an enduring relationship?

Experience economy

Another change in my perspective is that IT service management will never be a 'pure' experience as Pine and Gilmore describe in their book The Experience Economy. Whereas many attractions at Disney World can be replaced by other attractions without fundamentally changing the experience that attracts millions of people, if you need a sales system, it can't be replaced by an HR system. It's primarily about the content, but the experience can make it or break it.

To quote the Elevating the IT Service Experience white paper that I wrote for AXELOS, IT organizations can, however, adopt and adapt practices from organizations for which experience is the primary value driver. The experience tipping point in enterprise IT is not when experience becomes *more* important than the underlying services, but when it is of *significant* importance. In these cases, providers that play to both the consumer's rational and emotional needs not only co-create more value but also have a competitive edge.

Digital and IT services are now too important for technology to outweigh humanity. Experience is not only a commercial value driver – it also improves our emotional state, leading to better well-being for all involved, and business impact in terms of motivation and performance. In good IT service design, outcome prevails over output, and touch prevails over tech.

A.8 Other XLA publications

Although publications about IT service management increasingly refer to the importance of the service experience, there are not many books that focus on XLA. This appendix contains an overview of what I am aware of, in chronological sequence.

Digital Empathy: When Tech Meets Touch, by Marco Gianotten (2017)

Provocative reading by one of the XLA pioneers in the early stage of the 'movement' this short book is mostly about the need for a different approach, with some high-level thoughts on what to do but not much om how to execute. The content is still valid but most of it is incorporated in the XLA Pocketbook where it is better structured and more detailed.

Table of contents

- Digital empathy - why there's no getting away from it
- Chapter 1 - heading towards an IT crisis?
- Chapter 2 - the ingredients of it - new style
- Chapter 3 - experience first with the XLA
- Acknowledgements
- Notes
- Reading list
- Index

XLA Pocketbook, by Marco Gianotten (2023)

I was this book's content editor and influenced the structure and codification of the content. I am therefore biased but it's a fair statement that this is the first coherent overview XLA in a single publication. It introduces the concept of XLA and the XLA 6P Framework for understanding and applying IT service experience management. It is intended for IT service providers and consumers who want to learn the basics of XLA in order to derive more value from IT services. The underlying assertion is that investment in IT service experience and its business impact fosters more meaningful, rewarding, and productive work.

The XLA Pocketbook includes examples of the application of XLA, an introduction to the XLA 6P Framework, an overview of the key XLA concepts, an XLA template, and Giarte's glossary of XLA terms.

Table of contents

- About this book
- Chapter 1 - Introduction to XLA and the XLA 6P Framework
- Chapter 2 - Business case for better IT service experience (why)
- Chapter 3 - IT service experience and its management (what)
- Chapter 4 - Organization of IT service experience management (who)
- Chapter 5 - Transformation of the IT service management organization (how)
- Glossary

Chapter 1 gives a history of XLA and introduces the XLA 6P Framework that provides a way of thinking (perspectives), a way of working (practices and products), and a way of being (people, principles and propositions).

Chapter 2 is about the importance of co-creating value with customers through IT service management. It proposes the Xperience Level Agreement as an effective instrument through which to improve customer value.

Chapter 3 is about the increasingly higher demands people place on
providing and consuming IT services and explains how a better IT service experience has a positive business impact.

Chapter 4 describes the organizational structure and other resources needed to adopt and practice IT service experience management as an integrated part of IT Service Management.

Chapter 5 describes an approach for adopting IT service experience
management and embedding it into IT service management activities.

Completely Satisfied, by Hank Marquis (2023)

This book is about capturing and improving digital employee experience. Hank writes in refreshingly short and clear sentences. No fluffy preamble but upbeat and actionable guidance, using cases to support his points. He uses constructs such as RATER (Reliability, Assurance, Tangibles, Empathy, and Responsiveness) that are simple to understand, but not simplistic and in denial of the complex and intrinsically unpredictable nature of service.

Hank makes bold assertions that will get you thinking. These are not made in ignorance of what has already been said about IT satisfaction — he has done his research. He makes regular reference to, and builds on, well-established frameworks such as SERVQUAL.

His '10-step experience satisfaction process' is by far the biggest part of the book and contains many plausible actions to consider incorporating in an experience improvement journey.

Table of contents

- Introduction
- What satisfaction is and is not
- The 10-step experience satisfaction process
- Experience satisfaction in action
- Conclusion

Acknowledgements

A word of appreciation for Akshay Anand, David Barrow, Roman Jouravlev, Sakari Kyrö, Hank Marquis, Roman Pelzel, Doug Rabold, René Visser, Ronald Vrkić and Peter Wiggers for their generously critical feedback on a draft of the manuscript. Their astute observations resulted in a better book.

Printed in Great Britain
by Amazon